A PSYCHIC STUDY OF THE MUSIC OF THE SPHERES

Other books by D. Scott Rogo

A Psychic Study of the Music of the Spheres

Vol. 2 of Paranormal Music Experiences

By D. Scott Rogo

Anomalist Books
San Antonio • New York

To the memory of Professor Ernesto Bozzano,
   Who first brought attention to this phenomenon

To Dr. Robert Crookall,
   Who laid much of the foundation work upon which this
   volume is based

                            and

To my teacher, Dr. George Skapski,
   Professor of Music, California State University, Northridge

Contents

Foreword

This book, as well as its predecessor and companion work, *NAD: A Study of Some Unusual "Other-World" Experiences* (New Hyde Park, N.Y.: University Books, Inc., 1970), is an extremely valuable pioneering study of a most extraordinary psychical phenomenon—paranormal music. The subject, prior to Rogo's investigations, has been neglected, in spite of its obvious importance to psychic science. It is of particular importance to research into survival of death and "astral projection," or OOBE (out-of-the-body experience) phenomena. Scott Rogo has dealt masterfully with this field and has ably brought it into the clear light of scientific examination.

I have a particular interest in the phenomenon of paranormal music, since I had the great fortune to hear it (my experience was included in Rogo's previous study). The phenomenon is fact! From my personal experience I can assure the reader that the author has dealt with the subject in a splendid and complete manner. Its beauty is truly inconceivable and beyond description. The music of the greatest of earthly masters is childish and dissonant by comparison, and its true nature (in my case) is beyond conception. I cannot say, for example, whether

9

the music was either choral or orchestral—I do not think such terms really apply—and all one can really say is that its beauty was incredibly advanced over anything we can dream of. But I can affirm that Scott Rogo has dealt with this effect in a most thorough and scientific manner.

A number of cases involving paranormal music are given in this work which, when added to the cases included in his previous book, provide a large number of illustrative examples of this phenomenon. Interestingly, a typical example, if such term can be properly applied, listed in this book was described by Edward Randall, a noted lawyer who experimented for twenty years with Mrs. Emily French, the famed voice medium, who was also studied by Dr. Isaac Funk.

A criticism which has been leveled at the study of paranormal music is a direct doubt that such a phenomenon actually represents anything more than a subjective effect, a kind of auditory hallucination. Rogo has countered this suggestion in a most decisive and thorough manner.

First, he has pointed out that, by the use of pattern analysis, various patterns have been revealed which were previously totally unknown. Obviously, when highly individual trends are discovered and general patterns are established, mere chance cannot be invoked in "explanation." Needless to say, the use of content analysis is a widely known and thoroughly legitimate procedure used in science. As Rogo has noted, it is surprising to find that criticism has been advanced against the concept of paranormal music which completely ignores—or misses—the proper and legitimate use of this scientific procedure. It can be stated, then, that the reality of this phenomenon has been well established as a major psychical manifestation.

Rogo further notes that such music has in certain cases been heard collectively—by more than one witness. Clearly, when a phenomenon which has been properly witnessed is experienced collectively, then the criticism that it is hallucinatory in nature no longer can be invoked.

Rogo has noted that paranormal music occurs in several varieties. It exists as a separate phenomenon apparently unrelated to other factors; it is intimately associated with "astral projection" or out-of-the-body experiences; it is associated with the act of dying, and in this form was noted by Sir William Barrett and Professor Ernesto Bozzano; it has been heard during cases of haunting. In short, it takes several forms—all of which are listed and analyzed in this comprehensive book.

A most interesting discussion will be found which analyzes its relationship to the field of paranormal phenomena and mysticism.

An important section of the book is devoted to the question of exactly how paranormal music is "heard." Rogo points out that in cases, for example, where the music is heard collectively, different witnesses may hear the music in unlike modes. One case included a witness who heard, in the presence of a dying woman, music with voices, yet another witness heard the sounds of an "Aeolian Harp." The author concludes that paranormal music is not heard by our normal hearing process but is heard instead by what can be termed psychical perception.

Many points of the greatest importance are surveyed, including the fact that in spiritualistic literature, which represents communications from the dead, it is repeatedly observed that music plays a most significant part in the next world and that it bears a clear relationship to paranormal music of this existence.

The relationship of such music to survival of death and survival evidence is well explored, and Rogo demonstrates that it plays a most important role in the survival problem and can indeed be considered an integral part of survival phenomena.

Interestingly, the author includes a section which gives a selection of pseudo and doubtful music cases. When this list is studied, it quickly becomes apparent that false cases bear little relationship to the authentic phenomenon.

Again, I wish to state that I believe this book represents a very significant and pioneering study of a little-known psychical phenomenon of great importance, and that its value, of course,

lies in its case histories and particularly in its fascinating theoretical discussions.

Raymond Bayless[1]

.

---

[1] Raymond Bayless is the author of *The Enigma of the Poltergeist,*
Animal Ghosts, The Other Side of Death, Experiences of a Psychical
Researcher, and *Apparitions and Survival of Death.*

Preface

This volume is a sequel to my previous volume on psychic music, *NAD: A Study of Some Unusual "Other-World" Experiences,* published in 1970. However this book is a self-contained entity and the reader need not be familiar with my previous work to understand or appreciate the present monograph, even though the numbering of the cases picks up where the cases in *NAD* left off.

Unlike the first volume, which was, in essence, a casebook, the present volume is meant to relate the NAD phenomenon to the general outline of psychical phenomena. Because of this, references are given to cases in the first volume, but it is not necessary to be familiar with that catalogue of cases in order to comprehend the points I discuss here.

To avoid confusion I italicize the word *NAD* when referring to my first book, and use NAD in standard capital letters when referring to the phenomenon itself.

Although several appreciations are given in the acknowledgments, I would like to give special thanks to Mrs. Blanche Fortier, librarian of the Society for Psychical Research, for helping me procure copies of old cases in rare volumes, and to Renée Haynes for translating several of these cases from the French.

D. SCOTT ROGO

Canoga Park, California, 1972

13

Part I

Chapter 1

Introduction

Psychic music is one of the most unusual of all psychic manifestations. Not only have various individuals heard music, described as unbelievably beautiful and beyond any earthly music, which has no normal source, but this same music (if music it be), described in a similar fashion, has been heard during just about every known type of psychic experience. It has been perceived accompanying the appearance of apparitions, during the out-of-the-body experience (OOBE), and at death. It has manifested telepathically and in "haunted" houses. A formidable display—and only one basic generalization can be made: All the cases which were outlined in the first volume of this study, *NAD: A Study of Some Unusual "Other-World" Experiences* (New Hyde Park, N.Y.: University Books, 1970), are described in such identical terms that we may be assured that all the phenomena are interrelated and, in fact, represent different manifestations of *one* phenomenon.

This music was first termed "La Musique Transcendental" by the Italian psychical researcher Professor Ernesto Bozzano. He was the first to give this phenomenon due consideration in the scheme of psychical occurrences, and described it in his monograph, *Phénomènes Psychiques au Moment de la Mort*, which appeared in the 1920s. Since Bozzano's discussions pertained mainly to only one phase of the phenomena—music heard at deathbeds, as did also William Barrett's discussion of the music in his posthumously published work, *Deathbed Visions*—we suggested the Sanskrit word NAD (referring to the "audible life stream") as a more inclusive term to cover this music in all its many forms.

Our first volume had only one primary goal: to place NAD on the map (so to speak) of psychical phenomena, since Anglo-Saxon literature has rarely even mentioned the music—though there are numerous references to it in old spiritualist books, cases published by the Society for Psychical Research, and psychic autobiographies. Because of this scarcity of information, *NAD* was devoted almost exclusively to case studies of the phenomena, which were taken from first-hand witnesses (most of whom were interviewed by mail) and over forty historical sources. These sources ranged from as far back as the Dialogues of Saint Gregory and the S.P.R.'s monumental *Phantasms of the Living* (1889) to present-day accounts such as appear in *Fate* magazine and *Psychic News*.

However, since *NAD* was basically a casebook, several interesting aspects of the data were not discussed. In fact, NAD seems to be shaped like a delta—ever spreading but never completing its form. That is why this second volume is being presented. For, although we touched upon the basic theoretical implications of the phenomena, we did not devote space to the higher problems of the music. How is this music heard? What causes it, and what are the mechanics of the phenomenon? How does it fit into the general network of psychic phenomena? Is it objective, subjective, or (like the allusive apparition) somewhere between the two? Can we find new patterns indicative of the music, and now, having more cases to work with, can we verify the patterns we have already discovered? To these questions we turn now.

Of paramount importance, before an in-depth analysis of the case studies is made, is the question: How can we validate the phenomenon? When a person hears transcendental music, it is impossible to verify that the percipient did actually hear it. And certainly it would be hard to claim a supernormal cause for the music. One of the main criticisms of NAD was that few cases were well evidenced. This criticism is lame for two reasons: first, the nature of the phenomenon does not lend itself to this type of validation (William James was not criticized because the narratives in his *Varieties of Religious Experience* were not "well evidenced") and, secondly, it was *specifically* stated in NAD that the evidence for the validity of the phenomenon came from the use of content analysis—that if the phenomenon were genuine all the reports would fit into neat, though complex, patterns which would not be expected to occur by chance. Faked reports, on the other hand, would not have such general patterns unless all the percipients were in collusion. We did find such patterns, and content analysis is a perfectly legitimate scientific method. So it was surprising to find some of these criticisms based on the grounds that the book did not meet a criterion which it was expressly *not* written to meet!

What, then, is psychic music? And what relation does it have to "real" music? The following case points out very well the way in which the phenomenon manifests in its pure form—that is, not in adjunction to other phenomena, such as the appearance of an apparition or at a death.

Case No. 102 — Edward Randall

This case was narrated in a volume, *The Dead Have Never Died* (London, Allen & Unwin), which dealt with the mediumship of Emily French. The experience was of the author, Edward Randall. The music was heard during a camping trip in Canada. After a day of canoeing through the lakes which network parts of that country, he returned to the log cabin which was serving as his lodging:

> I sat down in a great chair on the veranda to rest. Soon the purple twilight came, and with it the silence that falls between toil and sleep. . . .

I was weary, and musing on the marvelous experiences that had been mine, my thoughts went out to my own, in the afterlife, and to the many new friends and acquaintances I have made among such people. [This was written shortly after Randall had been convinced of psychic survival through the mediumship of Mrs. French.] There was harmony between the eye and brain, the tints between earth and sky becoming neutral. I looked lazily upon the waters, at the islands and down the long bay and as I mused, there fell upon my senses music so distant as hardly to be perceptible. Was it music at all? I listened again; it seemed to be in a valley among the hills. I could not believe my senses, it was distinct yet not distinct, it sounded like a great orchestra of string and reed instruments played by master hands and with it the gentle wind among the trees and all the voices of Nature seemed to blend in one great whole; *it approached with soft cadence and then receded,* passing back into the silence where it was lost.

The narrative represents almost a perfect case of psychic music. The account, in fact, is almost identical in setting and observation to what was recorded by Bayard Taylor, the famous author [*NAD*, Case No. 18].

This report can illustrate two facets of the NAD phenomenon: (1) our method of analysis and (2) patterns indicative of the music.

1. I think it is obvious that no one could suggest that we try to give corroborative evidence for Randall's experience. Just as with "mystical experiences," the out-of-the-body encounter, and similar phenomena, the only standards we have by which to judge are the intrinsic quality of the observation (our second point of discussion) and the veracity of the reporter—a factor taken for granted in every science except parapsychology, though I certainly do not propose its use as the sole criterion.

2. The narrative also reports various details which, after analyzing over one hundred cases in our previous study, are in-

dicative of the music. It was described as a great orchestra (although usually the music is described as choral, when it is not, it is often described as an orchestra, with special attention given to the immensity of the sound). For instance, we find such comments as "produced by a vast number of players, singers" [Case No. 1], or "a very large group of instruments" [Case No. 17]. The music was said to have emerged from almost inaudibility to full volume and then receded. This we called the "crescendo" effect, and it was *the* most common pattern found in our cases. As I stated in *NAD*, page 33:

> Another important observation is the many references made to the crescendo effect of the music. Mrs. Powell recorded "the higher I got, the louder the music became" [Case No. 7]. Mrs. Palmer states that the music "swelled" [Case No. 11], and Mrs. Lehmann writes that the music swelled in intensity and then ebbed [Case No. 14]. James C. Edgerton heard the NAD "increase from zero volume which seemed to fill the Universe" [Case No. 6].

To this quotation we may add such comments as "the music was barely heard, but it steadily gained in volume . . . and then diminished until it faded out completely" [Case No. 1], and "the music appeared to be from a distance and then would gradually grow in strength" [Case No. 43]. To these we could add many others.

These are only two patterns indicative of the phenomenon. Indeed, as critics have pointed out, most of the narratives are not very detailed, so analysis is difficult. But if you were to hear the most incredibly beautiful music you ever heard (as a majority of the narrators report), could you be any more specific? Especially if you stated that the music was beyond anything mundane. Several narrators have tried to compare it to earthly music, and these fall into three genres: a huge choir, a large orchestral body, or the rolling sounds of an organ.

21

This, then, is psychic music. It is very unlike most other psychic occurrences and might be considered just a psychic oddity were it not that so many observations have appeared and are continuing to appear in psychic literature.

Chapter 2

Psychic Music: Its Various Manifestations

One of the unique features of psychic music is its affinity for manifesting in conjunction with other psychical occurrences. In our first study of some one hundred cases, only 21 percent heard the music in normal states of consciousness as a solely manifesting phenomenon. This is odd inasmuch as this same music was heard 19 percent of the time related to the out-of-the-body experience and 19 percent of the time as part of a deathbed vision. One might have thought the phenomenon would occur in its pure form at a much higher ratio than it would mixed in with other phenomena. However, the data show quite the contrary—that psychic music is heard equally often as a corollary to other phenomena.[1]

Because of this anomaly, before I discuss the more complex problems the phenomenon poses, it would be wise to present in abbreviated form a discussion of the various forms the music takes.

As was previously stated, NAD is often heard as a distinctly individual phenomenon. While we do not know what prompts

---

[1] These are rough percentiles figured from the cases presented in Chapters 1, 2, 3, 4, 7, and 8 of *NAD*.

the occurrences of the music, it often is heard at a time when the percipient is about to sleep, when he is deeply engrossed in nature or in contemplation, or in extreme depression. Similarly, it might be added, these are the times when OOBEs are prone to manifest.

Case No. 103 — Jesse Brookes

The case came to the author *in litt.* (December, 1970):

> My experience occurred nearly twenty years ago. I am not sure whether I had been sleeping or was just on the verge of sleep, when I began to hear this incredibly beautiful music. I have never been able to find words to describe it. . . .
> It so thrilled me that I felt about to burst, and at one time I seemed to rise up, to be floating. [This could have been an incipient OOBE.]
> At the time I was engaged in the business of selling phonograph records, so I knew what good music should sound like. To compare this celestial music to my best records would be like comparing a pipe organ to a sliding tin whistle. [Compare to Case No. 1: "The greatest music on earth, be it Brahms or Bach, is nothing but an inharmonious jangle of crude sounds by comparison."]
> While listening to the music the thought came to me, "Oh, if I only can get this on a phonograph record, my fortune will be made!" And abruptly the music stopped.

Case No. 104 — Attila von Szalay

> It was approximately during the mid-1930's as near as I can remember. I was very much the materialist at this time . . . a complete nonbeliever in anything psychic, spiritistic, or religious. I was walking down a hill smoking a cigar when suddenly I began to hear faint music in the distance. However, instead of actually being in the distance it was in my ears, in both ears,

24

sounding as does stereo today. . . . It seemed to be in my head. I just stood still and the music welled up into my consciousness; this is the only way that I can describe it. I became overwhelmed by it. I could not distinguish any particular musical instruments or any particular melody and I could not identify any human voices. I just stood there and the tears came into my eyes and I think that I became entranced, for at least ten minutes. I was oblivious to a crowd of people around me but I only became aware of them when I recovered from this state. There is no way of describing the music except to say that I was overwhelmed by something so majestic that any music heard here on earth is nothing, absolutely nothing in comparison to it.

It should be noted that, in just about all our cases, special mention was made that the music was beyond any earthly music. This raises an interesting point concerning the attempt to draw corollaries from these cases. Jule Eisenbud, M.D., one of the country's leading psychoanalysts as well as a parapsychologist, wrote to me that to describe the music as "indefinably beautiful" was nonoperative and too vague to be of any use in content analysis. He wrote:

What intrigues me is the idea of persons of all sorts of musical training and sensitivity, and from different musical epochs, all finding the celestial music "the most beautiful I ever heard!" If you questioned a dozen or a hundred persons today about what they considered "the most beautiful music" I am sure you would get a wide dispersion in the responses, everything from hillbilly music, through Sousa's marches, rock and roll, "Smoke Gets in Your Eyes," Beethoven's *Violin Concerto* and Bartok's *Violin Concerto*. What degree of objectivity to ascribe to these responses, all described as "the most," is hard to fathom. To me it sounds more like the responses a neurosurgeon would get if he placed electrodes in the hypothalamus and cortex together in the next twenty people upon whom he had occasion to operate. I am, of course, not really suggesting a neurological mechanism.[2]

I think that Dr. Eisenbud's point is a fair one, although easily rebutted. One of the remarkable consistencies of our data is that very few individuals have even tried to compare it with earthly music. Quite the contrary, many have independently stated specifically that the music was so far beyond the music of the great composers that their productions seem ludicrous by comparison. Although some narrators seek to describe the music in relation to certain musical media (choirs, orchestras, and so on), psychic music is practically never recognized in normal states and rarely in deathbed cases, as anything like what the music resembled in relationship to their own tastes or exposure (with rare exceptions, Case No. 29. See also a case of recognized music in the Countess Nora Wydenbruck's book, *The Paranormal* [Rider and Co., n.d.] pages 83–84). The important point is that the very many percipients all stated that the music was not only "*the* most beautiful they had ever heard," but "*beyond* what they ever heard." There is an important distinction here. Describing the music as "the most beautiful" would certainly be contingent on the musical tastes of the percipient, but stating the music was "beyond" what they have been exposed to is quite a different matter.

In describing the music as "beyond" earthly music, the percipients place NAD on a different level, and the tastes and predilections of the narrators become a superficial point. Because the vast majority of the narrators expressed the opinion that the music was beyond mundane creation, I find the interpretation of the cases contrary to Dr. Eisenbud's criticism. I feel that the unanimity of these remarks is astounding (even more so if the narrators *had* different tastes and backgrounds). They serve as a specific point of coincidence which is highly

---

[2] Private correspondence, January 13, 1971. The theory of a cerebral origin of the music will be discussed in a later chapter.

evidential . . . that all the percipients heard the same phenomenon of transcendental music which so impressed them that the love of their own favorite music was meaningless in comparison. Psychic music is heard during the out-of-the-body experience more often than with any other phenomenon. In fact, NAD seems to be so intricately related to the OOBE that later on we will discuss the relationship and its significance in depth. Cases such as the two following are rather indicative:

Case No. 105 — Kathleen Knutson

This case was originally published in *Fate* magazine, July, 1969:

> By the spring of 1936 multiple sclerosis had taken from me the power to walk. On October 10 that year I lay in my twilight-darkened bedroom in our home in Redgranite, Wisconsin, knowing little more than that my mother and father were sitting beside my bed. . . . I heard a door close; then all was quiet.
> *From some distant realm came music and a kaleidoscopic glow of light.* Slowly my body seemed to float up toward the light. . . . Slowly the light dimmed into the lamplight of my room. I felt a new buoyancy and the semicoma seemed to lift. When the doctor finally arrived at my bedside I was feeling better than I had for weeks.

Case No. 106 — A Polio Victim

This case represents a much more complex experience. Oftentimes the percipient not only feels that he has left the body but is projected to "the other world" and sees deceased relatives and friends. Dr. Robert Crookall, who has made extensive analyses of the OOBE in his several volumes on the phenomenon, has determined from his many case histories that in cases where the OOBE was catalyzed by illness, near death, or in a normal state, the "change of environment" appears in 14.5 percent of the recorded studies (based on 214 reports).[3]

The following case also stems from *Fate* magazine (August, 1950). The incident was reported by the girl's nurse, Virginia Randall. After being confined to an iron lung for six months, the girl recovered and described one of the experiences as:

> . . . a wonderful floating feeling. I could walk again, my muscles could do what I wanted them to do and I felt completely happy. I was so pleased to leave my worn-out shell behind me and be free. A bright light attracted my attention and I moved toward it. As I slowly approached it, I found myself in a new world [floating toward a bright light is an indicative experience during the OOBE].
> A soft diffused light—not like harsh sunlight—glowed and everything was joyful . . . soothing, minor chord music came an unseen orchestra, and all the people I saw were smiling and happy looking.

After seeing many of her deceased relatives, she continues:

> Then very suddenly a light appeared—a great Golden glory that was so dazzling I couldn't look at it. We all hid our faces and *from out of the music swelling from the light* came a wonderful voice. . . . The voice spoke to me: "No, Dorothy, I am sorry, but it is not time yet. You have more to do down there." [This command is often heard during the OOBE. In Crookall's studies we find remarks such as Case No. 180: "You cannot stay here, you must go back"; Case No. 25: ". . . was told to live the rest of my life"; and Case No. 343: "It is not your time yet—you must go back. You have work to do."]

[3] Crookall, Robert: *More Astral Projections* (London: Aquarian Press, 1964), p. 146.

If music heard during the OOBE is one of the most prolific forms of the NAD manifestation, music heard at deathbeds is certainly the most varied.

Deathbed music has two features not associated with music heard during the OOBE or in normal states. For one, the music may become audible not only to the percipient but collectively among all the witnesses as though it were an objective phenomenon [Case Nos. 39–44]. As may easily be seen, music heard in our other categories represents subjective experiences unfolding only to one individual. The fact that deathbed music has been heard collectively is the reason it is the only form of NAD that has found its way into psychic literature through the work of Bozzano and Barrett. Its value lies in the reality that we now have a multitude of witnesses and we can compare their testimonies and observations—often with surprising results, as we shall see in the chapter, "Psychic Music: Sense Perception or Psychic Perception?" This is not a general rule, for we still have many cases wherein the dying person alone heard the music [Case Nos. 36–38].

The second unique feature of deathbed music is that sometimes the music has been recognized and appears to be more of an earthly nature, though the witnesses still place it above worldly music. This feature is coupled with the fact that, in some cases, deathbed music has been, at first, thought to be of normal origin, but then discovered to have no source [Case Nos. 34 and 42].

Case No. 107 — An Old Sailor

A good example of a subjective experience at death is related by Dr. John Mjoen, head of a sanitarium in Oslo, Norway. The case is one of a pseudodeath wherein the percipient seemed to have died and then revived. Mjoen, called in to attend an old sailor in coma, gave him a camphor injection. On reviving, the man stated, "You shouldn't have awakened me, doctor, I was experiencing a wonderful sensation. *It was all shining blue*

29

ocean and marvelous music. I never felt so well before" [from David Knight's *The ESP Reader*. New York: Grosset and Dunlap, 1969; original source not given]. The report does not state whether the sailor permanently revived.

One case which did end with the ultimate death of the percipient follows and was used by Sir William Barrett in *Deathbed Visions*. Again the music was subjective:

Case No. 108 — Daisy Dryden

The original report first appeared in the *Journal* of the A.S.P.R., Vol. XII, No. 6, and also was reported in H. A. Dallas's volume, co-authored with Vale Owen, *The Nurseries of Heaven*. The case dates from 1864. The percipient was dying of fever. A few days before her death she started seeing visions and announced that she was about to die. The amazing point of the case is that Daisy described the dead children of some of her visitors in great detail—children she had never seen in life. Before she died she told her father, "Oh papa, do you hear that? It is the singing of the angels. Why, you ought to hear it, for the room is full of it, and I can see them, there are so many [apparitions]; I can see them miles and miles away."

As we stated in *NAD*, deathbed music more times than not is described as choral.

The next few examples demonstrate NAD's property of becoming more objective and collectively heard, and thus more earthlike.

Case No. 109 — Ada G.

This is one of the few cases which were not originally recorded in psychic literature but appeared in the March, 1879, issue of the *Atlantic Monthly*. The case also found its way into Barrett's study:

> Mrs. G. with her two little girls, Minnie and Ada, of
> the respective ages of eight and nine years had been

30

staying in the country on a visit to her sister-in-law, but having taken a house near London, she sent the two children with their nurse off by an early train, following herself by one a few hours later. Towards the evening of the same day, one of the girls walked into the room of the house which they had quitted in the morning, where a cousin to whom she was much attached was sitting at his studies, and said to him, "I am come to say good-bye, Walter; I shall never see you again." The young man was greatly startled and astonished as he had himself seen both the little girls and their nurse off on the morning train.

At this very time of the evening both the children in London were taken suddenly ill, while playing in their new home, a few hours after they had arrived. They both died within the week, but the younger, Minnie, died first. The day after she was buried, the poor bereaved mother was anxiously watching the last hours of the one still left, for whom she well knew no chance of life remained. Suddenly the sick child woke up from a kind of stupor and exclaimed, "Oh, look, Mama, look at the beautiful angels!" pointing to the foot of the bed. *Mrs. G. saw nothing, but heard soft music which seemed to float in the air.* Again the child exclaimed, "Oh dear Mamma, there is Minnie! She has come for me! . . . At this moment Mrs. G. distinctly heard a voice say "Come, dear Ada, I am waiting for you!" The sick child smiled once again and died without a struggle.

This case is unusual in that it is not recorded that the child herself heard the music. Compare this to Case No. 100, where Lady C. saw an apparition, while Miss Z. T., seeing nothing, reported hearing a fleeting strain of music.

Case Nos. 110 and 111 — Reported by D. D. Home

A clear-cut example of the collective qualities of the deathbed music is recorded in D. D. Home's *Incidents in My Life* (published in the 1860s). Home, the famous physical medium,

31

reported music collectively heard at the death of his wife and, in the second part of his autobiography, at the death of his daughter.

During the illness of his wife, "Distant musical sounds were now heard every night in our room and on more than one occasion the singing of a bird was heard for more than an hour over her bed." Mrs. Howitt, also at the deathbed, recorded, "Frequently also during the first three months and the last two months of her illness, not only she, but all those around her heard delicious strains of spirit music, sounding like a perfect harmony of vocal sounds. During the last month the words were most distinctly heard, and were recognized as the chants for the dying in the Russian church."

This case well illustrates the faculty of the music to be actually recognized, so rare in other manifestations of the music.

When his daughter died, Home reported, "At the moment of her parting [April, 1872] from this world, we, and all the others present, heard as it were a hail of tiny sounds on the pillow where the beautiful little head rested. In every part of the room we heard also the sounds of music and of voices."

Not all such cases are as antiquated as these. In the German journal, *Zeitschrift für Parapsychologie*, March, 1933, comes the following report:

Case No. 112 — A Pious Girl

On the evening of the death of a kind pious girl some wonderful music was heard in the corner of the stove. The same thing occurred Sunday afternoon after she had died. No normal origin could be found.

NAD heard in normal states, during the OOBE, and at death represents the chief manifestations of transcendental music. Later we shall discuss the interrelationships of all these three genres.

Allied to these forms of NAD is music heard which apparently is more earthly. While not as vivid as the various cases cited above, music of a type similar to what we have been discussing has occurred in haunted houses, with mediums and in the presence of mystics.

Music heard in haunted houses usually does not match the magnificence of NAD as it manifests at other times, though there are some cases wherein the music heard does appear to be the celestial music we have been examining.

Case No. 113 — Castleconnell Castle

The little we know of this haunting and its music comes to us from a letter dated 1640 describing the haunting of a castle in Limerick, Ireland, belonging to Lord Castleconnell (in A. R. G. Owen's *Can We Explain the Poltergeist?* N.Y.: Garrett Publications, 1964):

> For news we have the strangest that ever was heard of enchantments in the Lord of Castleconnell's Castle, four miles from Limerick, several sorts of noise, sometimes of drums and trumpets, sometimes of curious musique with heavenly voices.

Music was also reported during the famous Hinton Amptner haunting. And music has been heard with mystics as well. In 1686, reports were recorded of music heard with Isabel Vincent.

Case No. 114 — Isabel Vincent

The pamphlet on this case was printed in 1689 and describes Isabel Jurieu, the Shepherdess of Saor, in Dauphine, who:

> . . . since February last hath sung Psalms, prayed, preached and prophesied about the present times in her trances. And upon the wonderful and portentous trumpetings and singing of Psalms, that were heard by thousands in the air . . . in the year 1686.

While this case is old, nineteenth-century cases of music heard with mystics could also be cited [Case Nos. 84, 85, 62].

33

These then are the principal manifestations of psychic music. Although diversified in the manner in which they occur, they are all aspects of one great phenomenon. Now that we have outlined the main features of the music, we can go on to discuss more complex instances and speculate on the nature of this phenomenon—its origin, mechanics, and significance.

Part II

An Index of Cases

Introduction

Before proceeding with our discussion of the significance of psychic music, its relevance in the general scheme of psychical phenomena, and theories about the nature of the phenomena, we will present a large body of cases of the same nature as those presented in *NAD*. These cases are chiefly the results of a survey of cases made through *Fate* magazine. The request was made only for readers to send in their experiences with psychic music.

Of prime interest was the desire to compare the cases in *NAD* to the present ones. The firsthand experiences in the previous volume were collected principally in Great Britain through a similar appeal in *Psychic News*. Of course, our other main source was cases found in the literature of psychical research, but these too were taken mainly from British sources, such as *Phantasms of the Living*, Crookall's books on the out-of-the-body experience, and so on. The main concern was to compare patterns found in the U.S. cases with those discovered in British ones. As one can see in reading the following reports there are no qualitative differences between the two sources of reports. This is a verification that our original observations and analyses were not at fault and also answers the criticism that our analyses were based on insufficient data.

One will also note that the quality of cases in the present volume is somewhat higher than the firsthand accounts in *NAD*. This is not to imply that the U.S. survey was necessarily of a higher order. When *NAD* was written, virtually nothing was known about the phenomena and it was necessary to include in the book most of the cases received since we could not compare incoming cases to any previously set standard. However, with this second appraisal these matters have changed. We now have a firmer foundation from which to evaluate new cases. Thus the firsthand cases in the present volume represent a much higher level of selectivity. All told—about 50 percent of the reports in the U.S. survey were disqualified for such diverse reasons as (1) lack of detail, (2) obvious fabrication, or (3) inconsistencies in the report.

NAD was criticized for lack of detail in many cases, and admittedly the criticism is justified. However, in working with only the data at hand, having no previous basis from which to judge, this was inevitable. In the following study of cases we have included those which give more detail. Oftentimes the accounts were spread out in two or three letters, since considerable correspondence was carried on with the percipients. In some instances the quotations have been taken from more than one letter, as is stated in the accounts themselves.

(Readers will note a discrepancy in numbering. Because this section is technically a glossary, the numberings begin with Case No. 127, thereby skipping quite a few case numbers. Those cases, representing Nos. 115–126 will be found in subsequent chapters.)

Type I — NAD in Normal States of Consciousness[1]

Case No. 127 — Ross L. Bralley
(Ozark, Missouri)

---

[1] Italicized sections represent descriptions common to other cases.

The following account was received in a personal communication:

> Years ago around 1930 I was doing some door-to-door work for a small publishing concern and I was in a small town either in Oklahoma or Kansas and it was necessary to walk across a cemetery or go a block around to some steps. My mind was not on anything unusual, when suddenly as I was crossing the cemetery I both seemed to hear and feel the most beautiful singing. It seemed to be a choir or an audience singing songs of praise such as church audiences do. *However I did not recognize any earthly song I ever had heard. It was of a nature I find hard to describe. It was beautiful, no false strains or chords, blending perfectly in harmony with a perfect ethereal tone I had never heard before.* . . . It seemed rather distant yet near. I felt it and heard it. I stopped and listened for a time. I walked slowly out of the cemetery and *it seemed to fade and disappear. There were no earthly tunes I could recognize.* They were more beautiful and perfect than any I ever heard before.

Case No. 128 — B.R.G. (Macomb, Illinois)

In our first volume we cited a case (No. 25) where music was heard during childbirth. (There are several cases on record where childbirth also produced an OOBE.) The following case is of the former type and shows the relationship of the two phenomena, since the incident could have been an incipient OOBE:

> In 1942 when I was on the labor table trying unsuccessfully to give birth to my first child I had been scolded and admonished for what seemed to be hours of agony. Finally I gathered my all and on a wave of pain braced my feet and pulled on the handholds to the best of my ability. Nothing happened—as I was

39

sure it would not, but I knew I had done my best so I let myself go limp and drifted away from my tormentors [the doctors and nurses in attendance]. It was at this time I heard what I always afterwards referred to as "the beautiful music." I believe I knew what it meant because I remember looking up at the clock on the wall and thinking, "I'll be dead in a little while."

Mrs. G. on subsequent inquiries described the music as "light and beautiful." *"The music began very softly and became —not louder—but more clear as I turned my consciousness toward it.* It ceased rather abruptly as my mind focused on the doctor's voice."

Case No. 129 — Joan Sanford (Elkhorn, Wisconsin)

The family had retired for the night. My children were quite young then.

I awoke suddenly, listening. My husband was sleeping soundly beside me. I heard something—not sure at first what it was I was listening for. *Then, faintly as in a distance I heard music. It became louder.* I got out of bed and went to the open window. There was a gentle breeze, but not enough to cause "singing in the wires."

I knelt before the window resting my arms on the window sill, waiting. *I heard voices singing and instruments playing such music as I had never heard before. It was celestial in its beauty.* A heavenly chorus and orchestra. The sound was definitely coming from outside, not from any radio, *besides there has never before nor since been a sound like that coming from any radio, that I have ever heard.* I felt that it was almost directly overhead.

On inquiry Mrs. Sanford said she did not remember how the experience terminated but added that the next day, on questioning other people, she ascertained that no one else had heard the music.

Case No. 130 — Rosemary Mormelo
(Westfield, New Jersey)

It was the summer of 1947. I was living in East Orange, New Jersey, with my Aunt and Uncle. . . . This weekend the family was going out of town and I was to spend the weekend with another cousin of mine. My aunt didn't want to leave a seventeen-year-old girl all alone, she felt it wasn't safe. It was about 11:30 when I got out of the movies a few blocks away and I decided it was too late to go to my other cousin's, I would sleep home and take the bus first thing in the morning. As I unlocked the front door and stepped into the living room the whole room smelled so sweetly of flowers. I stood there trying to figure it out when I heard this beautiful music filling the room. I can only describe it as sounding like "angels singing."

Mrs. Mormelo, in a subsequent letter, gave a more detailed description of the music:

> The music seemed to come from everywhere in the room, filling every corner. *It was singing and yet there were no words. It was like a whole choir of sweet high voices that I can only describe as "angels singing."* It gave the feeling of something sacred and holy. [Several percipients report that they associated the music with religious things.]

Case No. 131 — Mrs. Carl MacComber
(Ladysmith, Wisconsin)

I was sitting in a small room opposite the living room. My old family grand piano was in my direct view. My old family violin without strings was on the piano.

Directly over these instruments close to the ceiling soft music began to be heard. *It was indescribable and lovely beyond compare. . . . The sounds swelled for several minutes then died away.* I tried to hum this music, but I could not get it down to my mouth. Again and again I tried. I could remember it, but not control it.

Case No. 132 – Betty Madison (Carson City, Nevada)

In Columbus, Ohio, when I was sixteen years old, I took a nap in the living room. As I awoke I heard faint strains of music. [Compare to Case No. 129.] I was thinking of turning the radio up louder when the *music increased in volume*. Then I knew it was not from this earth. It was a blend of several timbres but only a bell-like sound was identifiable. . . . *It was indescribably beautiful.* Time was suspended. *It faded away.*

To be sure that I had not mentally distorted earthly music I looked in vain for an earthly source. The radio was turned off, the only neighbors were not home and no sound came from their house.

Case No. 133 – Becky Schaeffer (Torrance, California)

This case also represents music being heard upon waking from sleep. While it may be argued that all cases of this type are actually hypnopompic illusions, such images do not have the intensity of these accounts nor do they last the duration which these cases report. However, this case might have been a hypnopompic illusion but its similarity to other cases warrants its inclusion here:

About two years ago I was involved in learning the art of meditation and found that it was a tremendous help in promoting serenity as well as improving the value of sleep. One morning I woke up as the last phrases of the most beautiful music were fading away. The regret at the loss, the tremendous "pull" to get back where the music was coming from are hard to forget. [This statement is similar to what is described by persons having OOBEs in normal states as well as near death. The present account might be the faint

42

recollection of an unconscious OOBE during sleep, which included hearing music. Such cases have been recorded in several instances. See *NAD*, Chapter 2.]

Mrs. Schaeffer adds the following remarks, which would indicate that the music was not an illusion: "The real time involved in consciousness of the music I described could have been little more than thirty seconds. But there was also a memory of having been immersed in it for considerable time prior to awakening."

The following four cases have one singular feature in common: NAD was heard while driving in an automobile. Because of this feature it is doubly interesting to compare the patterns involved.

Case No. 134 — Mabel Fulcher (Yarnell, Arizona)

In the twenties we [Mrs. Fulcher and a friend] were going home to a ranch at the foot of the San Francisco Peaks, five miles northwest of Flagstaff, Arizona, in the wee hours of a perfectly beautiful morning, after having danced the whole night through. We were driving along a rough and unpaved road when *suddenly just above me I heard music like I have never heard before.* I turned to my companion and inquired if he heard it. He didn't. . . .

In the thirties, I was in the desert near Wickenburg, Arizona. It was a bright sunny day and I was walking up a canyon with a lady companion when, *just above me,* I again heard this heavenly music. She could not hear a thing. I sat down on a rock and listened for about ten minutes to that "out of this world music."

In response to my letter asking for a more detailed description, Mrs. Fulcher wrote:

. . . *it was not like anything I have ever heard before.*
. . . *It always began rather softly and became quite*

43

loud. And it always stopped suddenly after fifteen or twenty minutes. [This is uncommon, the music usually is described as "fading away." However a sudden shifting of attention might cause an abrupt cessation of the music.]

Case No. 135 — Florence Ramsey (Thompson, Ohio)

The evening I heard the music while driving I was returning home from a Grange meeting and I was alone. I became aware of this music. *This was a choir of voices* and mixed both male and female. I assumed it was coming from the radio, which I thought had not been completely turned off when my son had last used the car. I never turned on the radio while driving as it is disconcerting. The music was so extraordinary I reached over to turn the knob and make it louder and then realized the radio was not even turned on. [The music] . . . *just faded out. The "voices" rose and fell, yet no words could be distinguished,* as though coming from a great distance. *They were uniform at all times. I could not recall the melody after it stopped yet it was fantastically beautiful* and so comforting somehow. . . . The words were not at all distinguishable, merely a blending of male and female voices, singing in a great choir.

Case No. 136 — Carl LaPat (Yarnell, Arizona)

I can't tell you the exact date this thing happened to me but it has been possibly a year and a half ago. . . . I was driving quite fast towards home. . . . I must have dozed off somehow and *what I can never forget is the most marvellously beautiful music I have ever heard....*

I've always liked fine symphonic, organ recitals, and other so-called "long-haired" music, so I know good music when I hear it. *But this that I heard was utterly beyond description, so heavenly, like angels singing,* accompanied by beyond-this-earth type of what? Perhaps organs? *That music became louder and louder* and I came to. [Mr. LaPat adds that coming back to consciousness kept him from a serious accident.]

Case No. 137 — Nellie M. Pattison (Scotts Valley, California)

Notice how this following case is almost identical to Case No. 135:

> I was driving along to work one day in the foothills of Saratoga—then I heard it—*the most beautifully heavenly music we could possibly hear and so very soft,* you had to really concentrate to hear it.
>
> By instinct I reached down to turn the radio higher . . . but realizing I had no radio in this car, I stopped the car, rolled down the window, but it [the music] did not come from anywhere but inside the car. I sat in complete awed rapture when I realized what I was hearing. It only lasted a very short time, but what a great thrill.
>
> The music started to fade a few moments only after I lowered my thought vibration in trying to find a means in which to better hear the music that was so delicious to the senses.

Mrs. Pattison adds that she thought the music was predominantly orchestral.

The reader can see the amazing concordance between these reports. The predominant description of the music is choral, often described as "angels singing." As we stated in *NAD*, this represents the most perfect form of the music. The reason for this is discussed in the chapter on how psychic music is heard. Also note that, just as with our English survey, the most striking pattern is a crescendo-decrescendo of the music. In fact, there is no difference at all in the content of the two surveys.

Type II — Out-of-the-Body Experiences

Case No. 138 — John Huntley

This case was recorded by J. Arthur Hill in his *Man Is a Spirit* (N.Y.: Doran Co., 1918):

About five years ago I woke from sleep to find "myself" out of the body. I was conscious of two places—in a feeble degree, in the body which was lying in bed on its left side; and to a far greater degree, away from the body (far away it seemed), surrounded by white opaque light and in a state of absolute happiness and security.

The whole of my personality lay "out there" even to the replica of the body—which like the body, lay also on its left side. I was not conscious of leaving the body, but woke up out of it. It was not a dream, for the consciousness was an enhanced one, as superior to the ordinary waking state as that is to the dream state. After lying in this healing light *I became conscious of what, for want of a better term, I must call music; gentle and sweet it was as the tinkling of snapping water in a rocky pool and it seemed to be all about me.* I saw no figure, nor wished to, the contentment was supreme. *The effect of these sounds was unutterably sweet,* and I said to myself, "This must be the voice of God." I could not endure the happiness, but lost consciousness there and returned unconscious to the body and woke next morning as though nothing had happened.

Case No. 139 — Mrs. M. E. Irvine

This case is taken from the same source (Hill).

When a child of fifteen years of age I was very, very ill and on the occasion I saw the most delightful vision. Where my spirit was I cannot say. . . . *But what I heard then has never left me—the music, oh, the music!* I shall never, never forget—I would gladly die tomorrow if I

46

could, if only to be able to hear what I heard and to see what I saw then.

Case No. 140 — Betty Madison (Carson City, Nevada)

Mrs. Madison's first account [Case No. 132] was recorded in the first part of this index. In her correspondence she also narrated another instance of hearing transcendental music, this time during an OOBE. The OOBE was caused by the percipient's experiments in meditation:

> ... After approximately three minutes I was near the ceiling by the north window that opened on the rear garden. The colors of everything were vivid and glowing. [This is commonly reported during OOBEs.] To my left came the same celestial music I described before. I did not see myself as having any form—no cord either. Time was suspended; suddenly I was on the bed again feeling my body as heavy.
>
> Again I searched for an earthly source of the music that I might have distorted but there was none.

Case No. 141 — Ivan Buffington (Bothill, Washington)

This OOBE was apparently caused by near-suffocation, which often causes the experience:

> In 1953 I was 19 years old and in the Air Force. I was stationed at a "remote" radio relay site just outside Choraw, South Carolina. It was my morning to put the station on the air. The sun had not yet risen and it was quite cool so when I went back inside the tent I lit the stove and put on water for coffee. I lay back down on my bunk. I apparently dozed off because the next thing I was aware of was music. *The music was growing very slowly louder.* The thing that struck me as unusual was that it was classical music (*I didn't recognize it as any particular piece*) and in South Carolina the only music on any radio station was "hillbilly." My first thought was

that it must be a car coming up the small dirt road that passed by the tent, so I roused myself to see who it was. As soon as I lifted my head from the pillow the music stopped abruptly. Thinking it must have been a dream I dozed off again. *The music started again very softly and began to increase in volume.* . . . The music did indeed continue to become louder and louder until it reached an incredible volume and suddenly reverted to one screeching continuous note [refer to Case No. 6]. At this point I opened my eyes and saw the light of dawn coming in through the window in the door but I couldn't focus my eyes, and every muscle in my body was rigid and seemingly resonating to the note I heard. I then had the sensation of withdrawing from my body, not getting up and leaving it but just backing away from it until I was some distance away and about 50 feet above it. I can remember the distance because all the time I was watching my own body lying there. Then as though someone were whispering over my shoulder I was informed I was dying. . . . The next thing I remember I was back in my body. My muscles were cramped and I couldn't breathe. I tried to holler to the guy in the next bunk but I couldn't even squeak, as there was no air in my lungs. Finally I was able to breathe again. The music stopped for the last time when I returned to my body.

Mr. Buffington wrote, in response to my question, that he was lying with his face buried in his hands, which probably caused near-suffocation producing the experience. Note how in this case *the music led up to the OOBE.*

Discussion: The NAD Experience— ### Paranormal or Mystical?

When we discuss psychical experiences we usually are discussing paranormal modes of "cognition." Telepathy is certainly the cognition of thoughts which are unchanneled by sensory means and are oftentimes locked deep within the unconscious. Clairvoyance is also cognition of definite data about material objects. In the NAD experience we do not have what can be called a cognizant experience. Indeed we do "perceive" something which is not heard by our normal senses, but can this be called a cognizant experience? It is hard to differentiate between what is higher perception and what is psychic cognition, and this might lead one to wonder if the NAD experience can be classified as truly psychical. The problem of NAD is similar to that of the mystical experience which one would hesitate to call a psychic experience. It is obvious that the NAD experience has psychical concomitants: Often it occurs corresponding to a death, and the music is recognized as heralding such an event. But in our conclusion we must determine what the nature of NAD is as an independent phenomenon.

In the light of the fact that so many mystics have had the experience, could NAD actually be more related to the mystical experience than the psychic? There is definite purpose in psychical experiences, usually the attempt to communicate knowledge when normal sense channels are not usable. There seems to be a primary motivation where psychical experience is involved. However, when we come to religious experiences, this element is lacking. As Edwyn Bevan wrote in his *Sybils and Seers*, such experiences, while profoundly affecting the percipient and having great value to him, have no meaning for anybody else. This is quite different from the purposefulness and teleological implications of psychic experiences. Now NAD, when perceived in the normal state, is certainly of the same category as undefinable religious and even mystical experience, and one might wonder if the basic essence of NAD is, in fact, more in the realm of mystical than paranormal experience.

Admittedly some have argued that the mystical and paranormal experiences do have some basic similarities: 1. The feeling of being "one with the universe," which typifies the mystical experience, is common to both mystical and psychical experience and has been recounted by persons undergoing the OOBE, by clairvoyants, and by mediums entering trance. 2. They have a

49

delayed emergence in normal consciousness, being sporadic and occurring only in certain circumstances. 3. Oddly, conditions that favor the mystical experience are similar to conditions which catalyze the paranormal experience. 4. Both experiences are extensions of our everyday consciousness. 5. The experience is normal to mankind. 6. Time and space are transcended. 7. Proof is many times beyond logical explanation. 8. People who undergo both types of experience have absolute certainty as to the reality of their experiences.[2]

The NAD experience fits into all of these similarities to some degree. Some people do feel that the experience has brought them closer to understanding the universe or at least a momentary feeling of transcendence (see Case No. 18). They do only rarely occur, thus the ability to have the experience seems to be deep within our own consciousness. A certain mental state seems to be necessary for the NAD experience to manifest. Certainly NAD is an extension of our normal modes of perception and so, an extension of our consciousness. The diversity of ages and cultures which have recorded NAD appears to show that it, although of a transcendental nature, is normal to man. Many experiencers described time as being suspended and many, during subsequent interviews, have specifically stated it would be impossible to determine the duration of the experience, while others have ventured approximations. Proof in many cases rests only in the certainty of the percipient who remains convinced of the "reality" of his experience.

Obviously NAD fits into the general criteria of psychic and mystical experience. But what makes the mystical experience unique?

The best categorization of the mystical experience is given by the philosopher W. T. Stace in his *Mysticism and Philosophy*

---

[2] See Robert Crookall's *The Interpretation of Cosmic and Mystical Experience* (London: James Clarke, 1969). An attempt to find common ground between these two was made in Lawrence LeShan's *Toward a General Theory of the Paranormal* (New York: Parapsychology Foundation, 1969).

(Philadelphia: J. B. Lippincott Co., 1960). Stace sees seven basic characteristics of the mystical experience:

1. Unitary consciousness
2. Nonspaciality and nontemporalness
3. Sense of objectivity
4. Feelings of blessedness
5. Feeling that the experience is holy
6. Paradoxicality
7. Ineffableness of the experience

Psychical experience does have some differences if we accept Stace's categorization. 1. While some persons undergoing certain psychic experiences do have feelings of unitary consciousness (at-oneness with all things), psychical experiences do not generally catalyze such feelings. Although some people feel, after a psychic experience, that the nature of the experience implies there is a basic unity to all life, the experience *usually* does not carry *direct and engulfing* realization or sensations of this unity during the actual experience. 2. Because of the cognizant nature of the psychic experience, which is a form of communication, the event is very much temporal. 3. While certain experiences of a psychic nature do bring with them feelings of objectivity, many times persons undergoing psychic manifestations will rationalize away the experience and later have doubts about it. This is not so with the mystical experience. 4. Very few consider a psychic experience as blessed. Although they might relate the occurrence to religious belief, the experience itself is not considered blessed or 5. divine. 6. Since psychical experiences seem to be controlled by certain variables, some of which are known, the paradoxical nature of the psychical experience has been somewhat removed. 7. Since psychic experiences usually do manifest in the form of sense perception, the experience is not ineffable.

How do NAD experiences fit into these characterizations? While affecting consciousness to a degree, the experience does not usually bring with it overwhelming feelings of unitary con-

51

sciousness. While it does bring momentary transcendence, this is a far cry from the mystical unity described both by mystics and common people who have undergone the experience. It is nontemporal in the fact that it is beyond any music of "this world," but the very fact that it can be described as music and manifests through a sensory channel ("hearing") places temporal requirement on it. While many persons hearing subjective NAD do most certainly consider the experience "real," they often have doubts about the etiology of the occurrence and try to find normal causes for it. This is wholly like psychic experiences and unlike religious feelings. Feelings of contentment and joy (4) do manifest and, while many relate the experience to religious things, they rarely consider the phenomenon a "blessed effect." Nor (5) do they consider the entire experience holy. Paradoxicality (6) is a common factor but (7) the fact is that, while describing the NAD in terms of "music," the percipients have no hesitations about describing the experience in worldly terms, thus disqualifying the phenomenon as truly ineffable.

By these comparisons one can see that the NAD differs from the category of mystical experience not by character but by degree. However, the key to classifying NAD comes from the two basic differences between psychical and mystical experiences: (1) Psychical experience usually manifests in the form of sense perception, and (2) definite information is cognized.

The NAD experience falls into both categories. NAD is heard as music, "other-worldly," but music nonetheless. In some cases, the experience is shared by a group of percipients. Mystical experiences are always *beyond* any semblance of sense perception, being "ineffable." And certainly no mystical experience was ever collectively shared. Secondly, while psychical experiences often have mystical concomitants, the mystical experience does not have psychical constituents. Although there are feelings of oneness with other living things, definite data are not given. While NAD in its normal state does not give any clear information, it has been known to impart implied knowledge (sometimes veridical) such as when percipients instinctively relate the music to a death. The mystical experience is so beyond sensory awareness that the "knowledge" gained by the experience is cosmic in nature and does not pertain to "this world" or even "the other world."

It is because of these factors that I feel that NAD is intrinsically a psychic experience. We cannot draw a definite line between the mystical and psychical, since both are extensions of our everyday awareness and our limited consciousness. NAD experiences do tend to fall into that gray area between the two but, nonetheless, NAD is a "property," to be sure, of another world, and when we compare the cosmic and psychic experience NAD falls nearer the realm of the latter.

An Attempt at Verifying the NAD Experience

Methodology

My basic procedure was to send out questionnaires to eleven percipients whose cases showed prima facie evidence of what I considered to be the NAD experience.[3] I did not want to include in the study (1) those percipients who had the experience in any other form than in "normal" states of consciousness (several cases on record occurred during the out-of-the-body experience), or (2) percipients outside the United States who might be unable to carry on lengthy correspondence.

Several questions were geared toward what the narrator "experienced" during the phenomenon. The other questions concerned subjective feelings about the experience. Of course, we should expect a higher conformity on the first set of questions. These questions were interspersed on the questionnaire.

The Questions and Their Results

1. The first object was to determine if there was any uniformity in the duration of the experience. Since most of the narrators wrote of the brevity of the experience, a "forced-choice" question was included asking the percipients to select from (a) shorter than one minute, (b) 1 to 5 minutes, (c) 5 to 15 minutes, (d) more than 15 minutes.

---

[3] Some recorded multiple cases.

The results were as follows:[4]

		Percent
(a)	Shorter than one minute	8
(b)	Between one and five minutes	55
(c)	Five to fifteen minutes	0
(d)	More than fifteen minutes	37

The results are not elastic, but fall into two significant patterns. The percentages are not randomly distributed, as would be expected if the experiences were illusory. As the results are of two kinds, it should be kept in mind that we may be dealing with two different types of the NAD experience.

2. Three questions were then asked concerning the volume of the music. Again a "forced-choice" situation was used requiring the percipients to choose between (a) soft, (b) moderately loud, (c) very loud.

The first question asked the percipients about the volume of the music at the *onset* of the experience. The results were as follows:

		Percent
(a)	Soft	73
(b)	Moderately loud	27
(c)	Very loud	0

Again conformity was found. I do not think this would necessarily be expected. My reasons for this opinion will become apparent in light of the next two questions.

The next volume-oriented question asked the narrators to describe the degree of sound at the *peak* of the experience, using the same categories as before. The replies were:

		Percent
(a)	Soft	18
(b)	Moderately loud	82
(c)	Very loud	0

---

[4] All these figures are rough, not exact, percentages (that is, they are rounded to the nearest whole percentage).

An even higher degree of uniformity is found. Finally, in answer to a question about volume of the music at the *end* of the experiences, we received these replies:

		Percent
(a)	Soft	63
(b)	Moderately loud	20
(c)	Very loud	0[5]

A general pattern may be seen emerging. The music began softly, made a crescendo, and then a decrescendo. When compiling my book, *NAD*, I became aware of this recurrent pattern. I do not think this could have been expected since, when I first asked for cases to be sent to me, I only requested that persons with *any* experience in psychic music should write to me. This request did not imply any specific form of the experience, and there was no reason to suppose that cases of music heard initially as a loud blast would not occur. Secondly, I expected, on the basis of my reports, that most percipients would choose category (c) as the volume when the music was at its peak. Instead, to my surprise, category (b) was most often chosen. Although some of my accounts do include the "crescendo effect" in the written report, most of the percipients only described the effect *after* I had written them a follow-up letter. Most of the original reports did not mention the effect at all. The greater number of the decisions as to which persons I would contact for this survey was made *before* the follow-up letters were sent, thus it cannot be argued that my decision to include these percipients was *due* to the crescendo-decrescendo effect. Even if this were the case, the high conformity of choice (b) (moderately loud) could not be explained, as the volume of the music at the height of the experience might well be expected (as it was by me) to be thought "loud."

---

[5] The percentages do not add up to 100 percent, since several percipients wrote in their reports that they either fell asleep before the experience ended or were distracted and did not remember what finally happened.

55

3. The next question dealt with a verbal description of the music. Since most of the percipients in *NAD* described the music as either choral, orchestral, or like an organ, I gave ten categories from which the survey group could choose:

(a) Choral—female
(b) Choral—male
(c) Choral—mixed
(d) Choral—undefinable
(e) Instrumental—strings

(f) Wind instruments
(g) Symphonic
(h) Choral and instrumental
(i) Like an organ
(j) Undefinable by any criterion

The results were as follows:

		Percent
(a)	Choral—female	8
(b)	Choral—male	0
(c)	Choral—mixed	16
(d)	Choral—undefinable	8
(e)	Instrumental—strings	8
(f)	Wind instruments	0
(g)	Symphonic	23
(h)	Choral and instrumental	8
(i)	Like an organ	0
(j)	Undefinable by any criterion	30

While this seems to be a random sequence, I do not think this fact in any way negates the general conformity of our cases, especially since we used such a small sampling. Also, it must be remembered that the average individual is not always qualified to differentiate among the sounds he hears. Since the NAD experience seems definitely not to be concerned with normally produced music (such as that produced by a radio) this adds to the confusion. As Professor Ian Parrott, a musicologist, stated in his review of *NAD*:

... A trained musician can fairly pick out the transient decaying sounds of plucked instruments or pianoforte, the inflexible sustained sounds of the organ, the pure tones or reedy sounds of woodwind instruments, the explosive initiations of the brass, the vibrato of strings, etc., but the general public, who record experiences, are usually only too vague on such technicalities. Are the impressions of "celestial" music sometimes purely projections of earthly musical sounds or is it something in its own right? Certainly the records given [in certain cases] suggest that they may be the former. However, the many accounts of the saints hearing bells and religious vocal music etc., suggest that celestial music may be getting an inadequate interpretation by the listener in terms which are of necessity of this world.[6]

I think this is an important point. This argument is well exemplified in a very well-documented case of collectively heard music investigated by Frank Podmore and Edmund Gurney, where all the percipients heard the music in different forms.[7]

I also categorized the results to see if there was a significant correlation between those percipients who had experiences of brief duration (shorter than five minutes) with certain musical types, and those with experiences by longer duration with other categories. While the smallness of the sampling makes it impossible to generalize from such a plan, there was a *suggestive* tendency for those who had short experiences to group their responses around (j) category (undefinable), while the answers of persons having long-duration experiences categorized the music much more randomly. However, the level of the randomness in ratio to the number of persons filling out the questionnaires keeps this tendency from being significant. A much larger survey would be needed to see if this tendency was general.

4. The following three questions were included to see if the percipients could isolate various properties of the music. They were: (a) Did the music have any definite melody? (b) Any

[6] Parrott, Ian: Review: "NAD, A Study of Some Unusual 'Other-World' Experiences," by D. Scott Rogo (*Journal:* SPR, Vol. 46, No. 747).

[7] Gurney, E.; Podmore, F.; Myers, F. W. H.: *Phantasms of the Living* (London: Kegan Paul, 1886).

definite rhythm? (c) Definite pitch or timbre? These were, of course, simple yes-no responses. The results were as follows:

	YES (Percent)	NO (Percent)
(a) Definite melody	46	54
(b) Definite rhythm	46	54
(c) Definite pitch or timbre	46	54

Since these percentages seem to be almost equally divided, I ought to note that the exact uniformity is a freak. Many percipients answered yes to one or two questions and no to the other or others. The statistics should not be presumed to mean that the replies were uniform.

Again, I thought it advisable to break down the answers in terms of those who had short-duration and long-duration experiences. The results are significant:

(a) Definite Melody:

	YES (Percent)	NO (Percent)
Short-duration experience	16	84
Long-duration experience	100	0

A clear division is seen. I do not think that the brevity of the experience can account for this significant correlation. Even if the experience was only one minute long, this would be adequate for the listener to determine a definite melody. For example the entire main theme of the last movement of the Brahms *First Symphony* is only thirty-two seconds long and the first strain of the Overture to *Tannhauser* is only forty-five seconds long.[8]

(b) Definite rhythm:

	YES (Percent)	NO (Percent)
Short-duration experience	30	70
Long-duration experience	75	25

Again a clear division is noticed.

---

[8] Based on recordings in my possession.

(c) Definite timbre or pitch:

	YES (Percent)	NO (Percent)
Short-duration experience	46	54
Long-duration experience	50	50

This third category is a bit confused, and I am afraid the confusion stems from my own vagueness. From the responses of those percipients which included written-in comments, I discovered that they were not sure of what I meant by timbre. Some did not even try to answer the question. However, I still think it highly significant that those with short-duration experiences uniformly denied the music had melody or rhythm, while those having longer-duration experiences did perceive melody and rhythm. This again is not necessarily to be expected, since long pieces of music (of, say, fifteen minutes) can be written without any perceptible melody or rhythm, relying solely on timbre (for example, Ligetti's *Atmospheres,* an orchestral work of this nature).

5. My final question, of a "forced choice" nature, attempted to determine the reaction of the percipients to their experiences. They were asked to select from the following categories: (a) fright, (b) awe, (c) bliss, (d) shock, (e) no reaction.

The reason for making a distinction between "awe" and "bliss" stems from the common usage of the term. "Awe" is used in regard to many psychic experiences, while the term "bliss" is commonly used to describe the mystic experience. The breakdowns were:

	Percent
(a) Fright	9
(b) Awe	54
(c) Bliss	36
(d) Shock	0
(e) No reaction	0

A significant group is found around categories (b) and (c). I had originally felt that this result was due to the fact that the percipients were really describing the same sensation. However, in breaking down these percentages in relation to short- and long-durational experiences, we find a distinct separation:

	Fright (Percent)	Bliss (Percent)	Awe (Percent)
Short-duration experience	15	15	70
Long-duration experience	0	75	25

A distinct difference is again seen between these two bodies of individuals. This was a very unexpected pattern.

6. The last question to determine any general consistencies was whether the percipient could tell if the music came from a fixed point in space or whether it was "all enveloping." There is general conformity:

	Percent
All enveloping	83
Fixed point	17

Several other questions were asked for my own interest. All the correspondents deny that they may have been dreaming or hallucinating. Most of them had never heard or read of the phenomenon before they experienced it. This question was included to determine whether the correspondents could have "borrowed" accounts from other sources. I doubt this, since the only major book on the phenomenon is my own, and most of the correspondents were surprised to discover that a book had been written on the subject. There was, however, no general consistency as to whether the experience was considered a religious one or not.

Discussion

I do not wish to spend time discussing the significance of these patterns or the interpretation of them. This I have done at great length in other sections of this book. However, I do think that my attempt to "validate" the experience is successful. In this discussion I would like to analyze two possible objections to my methods in making the statistical breakdowns.

The first objection is that the patterns demonstrated could

have been, in effect, self-fulfilling prophecies: that I specifically chose cases which fit into general patterns and then sent out my questionnaires. I am fully aware of the dangers of this type of misuse and have written on it elsewhere.[9] However, I think it valuable to point out that very few of the narratives originally sent to me gave any hint of the duration of the experience. I had no idea, nor could any idea be inferred from the accounts, that there were any over-all patterns concerning the length of the experience. The greater part of the most evidential material is based on the significant correlations between differences in short- and long-durational experiences. These could not possibly have been based on the reports I received in private correspondence.

Secondly, it could be argued that my sampling was too small for any conclusions to be reached. Of the eleven correspondents originally contacted, some reported multiple experiences, so that some of the questions were answered with a total count of more than eleven. In fact, a considerably larger number of experiences were used, but they came from just eleven percipients. It would be fair to make this argument if the percentages were not so staggeringly significant—but the level of uniformity on most of the questions could not be based on chance in even this small sampling.

I think it safe to assume that we are dealing with a very real phenomenon, which breaks down into two different types of experience—and I do not think chance can explain the inner consistencies always found in each category. Further, these consistencies would not have occurred unless all the narrators were having a similar experience. Thus I feel we have "verified" the NAD experience.

Type III — Cases Related to Death

We now come to the one area of psychic music that has been most written about in psychical research—deathbed obser-

<hr>

[9] Rogo, D. Scott: "Content Analysis as Evidence in Parapsychology" (*Parapsychology Review*, Vol. 2, No. 4).

vations. It was this body of cases that prompted Ernesto Bozzano to include "*la musique transcendantal*" as one of the most important psychic occurrences surrounding death. Sir William Barrett, in recognition of the importance of this type of case, used the data as part of his study of deathbed visions.

In this section we have included a larger body of cases than in either normal or out-of-the-body cases. The reason for this is not that they are any more common, but that they have in the history of psychical research been recorded more often, and in this section many cases from the literature of parapsychology have been included. This is by no means strange: Deathbed cases are the only ones that seem to have any veridical weight, being either (1) collectively heard, (2) related to a specific event such as death, or (3) observations of another person's experience. Thus, more cases are recorded and the chances of the experiences being due to illusion are narrowed considerably, giving greater weight to the testimony. No doubt many persons who have heard psychic music or undergone an OOBE have kept the experience guarded, rationalizing in their own minds that such sensations were illusions. It is only because certain rare individuals eventually become interested in psychical phenomena in general that their experiences finally surface.

In this section there are actually very few cases of deathbed music that have been received in personal communications. Again, this is in no way odd. Today, unlike the Victorian age or before, death largely takes place in a clinical setting. In past years death usually occurred in the patient's home with his relatives and friends around him. No doubt such a personal setting, so overlaid with emotion, nurtured such incidents as psychic music. But today death occurs in a hospital arena or nursing home, all too devoid of any meaningful setting. To some people it may seem odd to refer to death in terms of what is "meaningful," but there is no doubt that the starkness and sterility of the way modern society views death make it seem a fearful thing to many. It is not odd, then, that deathbed narratives such as the following are more unusual today. It is rare which psychical occurrences manifest. Also, doctors and nurses, enough that the dying are surrounded by loved ones, let alone in an atmosphere conducive to the delicate conditions under while they do report deathbed cases, are cautious in describing a phenomenon they themselves witness. Of our cases, only one (No. 34) occurred in a clinical atmosphere.

John Hinton, an English psychiatrist, in his book *Dying* has convincingly argued that our uncomfortable feeling regarding death has made it the terrifying "end" so many see it as. Robert Denniston of the publishing house of Hodder & Stoughton, in his introduction to an anthology, *Man's Concern with Death*, aptly placed the problem in its rightful perspective when he wrote that in contemporary society anything concerned with death "did seem like the new pornography—a secret and shameful matter totally opposed to the life-enhancing virtues of sex, love, freedom and immortality."

Unlike the Victorian age, contemporary society is very much regulated by a new hedonism. The Victorian era was largely governed, even if not consciously, by religious morals and ethics. In such a culture, where a religious faith had so much greater a bearing on individuals in society, it is no wonder psychical occurrences were reported around the time of death much more often than today. In trying to save man from death we have robbed it of much of its significance and beauty. As Ignace Lepp taught, death is one of man's most meaningful encounters.[10] And with that observation, we will go on to our study of deathbed cases and allied reports.

The lore of deathbed music is large and extends far back before organized research began. Wolfgang Goethe, the German philosopher, who seemed prone to psychical experiences throughout his life (1749–1832), was recorded to have died amidst the harmonies of transcendental music. Similarly, psychic music was heard by the child king, Louis XVII (1785–95), as

---

[10] Lepp, Ignace: *Death and Its Mystery* (From the French, Toronto: Macmillan, 1968. Originally published 1952).

recorded in the work *Vie, Martyr et Mort de Louis XVII* by A. Beauchesne, who took the original testimony from the witnesses.

Case No. 142 — Wolfgang Goethe

On the 22nd day of March, 1832, about 10:00 in the evening, two hours before Goethe's death, a carriage stopped outside the great poet's house. A lady got out and hastened to enter, asking the servant in a trembling voice, "Is he still alive?" It was Countess V., an enthusiastic admirer of the poet, who always received her with pleasure because of the comforting vivacity of her conversation. While she was going up the stairs she suddenly stopped, listening to something, then she questioned the servant, "What! Music in this house? Good heavens, how can anyone play music here on such a day as this?" The man listened in turn, but he had become pale and trembling, and made no reply. Meanwhile, the Countess had crossed the drawing room and gone into the study, where only she had the privilege of entry. Frau von Goethe, the poet's sister-in-law, went to meet her: The two women fell into each other's arms, bursting into tears. Presently the Countess asked, "Tell me, Ottilie, while I was coming upstairs I heard music in the house. Why? Why? Or was I perhaps mistaken?"

"So you have heard it too?" replied Frau von Goethe. "It's inexplicable! Since dawn yesterday a mysterious music has resounded from time to time, getting into our ears, our hearts, our bones." *At this very instant there resounded from above, as if they came from a higher world, sweet and prolonged chords of music which weakened little by little until they faded away.*

At this same moment, Jean, the faithful valet, came out of the dying man's room, much moved by the sounds and asked anxiously, "Did you hear it, Madame? This time the music came from the garden, and sounded just at the level of the window."

"No," said the Countess. "It came from the room beside us."

64

They drew back the curtains and looked out at the garden. A light and almost silent wind blew across the bare branches of the trees; you could hear, far away, the sound of a cart going along the road; but there was nothing to be seen which could explain the origin of the mysterious music. Then the two friends went into the drawing room, whence they thought the music must have come, but without observing anything unusual. While they were still busy searching, another series of marvelous harmonics was heard. This time they seemed to come from the study.

The Countess, going back into the drawing room, said, "I don't think I can be mistaken; it must be a quartet playing fragments of music some way off which reach us from time to time."

But Frau von Goethe for her part remarked, "On the contrary, it seemed to me that I was hearing the sound of a piano, clear and close by. This morning I was so sure of it that I sent the servant to implore my neighbors to stop playing the piano, out of consideration for the dying man. But they all said the same thing; that they knew very well what condition the poet was in, and were too much distressed to dream of disturbing his last hours by playing the piano."

Suddenly the music burst out again, delicate and sweet; this time it seemed to arise in the room where they were; only, for one person it seemed to be the sound of an organ, for the other a choral chant, and for the third [this sounds as if Jean, the valet, must have been with them] the notes of a piano.

A Mr. S., who was at that moment signing the medical report with Dr. B. in the hall, looked at his friend with surprise, asking him, "Is that a concertina playing?"

"It seems to be," the doctor replied. "Perhaps someone in the neighborhood is amusing himself."

"No," said Mr. S., "whoever is playing is definitely in this house."

It was thus that the mysterious music went on making itself heard up until the moment when Wolfgang

Goethe breathed out his last sigh; sometimes recurring after long intervals, sometimes after the briefest of remissions, sometimes in one direction, sometimes in another, but always seeming to come from the house itself or from quite close by; all the searches and inquiries undertaken to solve the mystery were in vain. [Taken from Bozzano's *Phénomènes Psychiques au Moment de la Mort.*]

Case No. 143 — Louis XVII

The time of the last agony drew near, and Gomin, one of the guards, seeing that the patient remained calm, silent, and motionless, asked him, "I hope you are not in pain?"

"Yes, I am still in pain, but not as I was before—this music is so beautiful!"

Not the slightest echo of music was to be heard. Moreover, none could be perceived in the room where the little martyr lay dying. Astonished, Gomin replied, "From which direction do you hear it coming?"

"It comes from above."

"And you have been hearing it for some time?"

"Ever since you knelt down. Don't you hear it now? Oh, let's listen, let's listen." And the child opened his great eyes, shining with ecstatic joy, and succeeded in making a sign with his bloodless little hand. The guard, moved, and not wishing to destroy this last sweet illusion, pretended to listen too. After a few minutes of close attention, the child seemed to tremble with joy, his eyes sparkled, and he said in a voice that expressed intense emotion, "I recognized my mother's voice among those who were singing."

Once this last sentence had come from the poor orphan's lips, it seemed to take away all suffering. His forehead became serene again; his gaze, calm once more, was fixed on something invisible. While waiting, one could see very well that he continued to listen with ecstatic attention to the harmonies of a concert beyond the range of human hearing. One would have said that the dawn of a new existence was beginning to brighten for this young soul.

Shortly afterward the other guard, Lasne, took over from Gomin, and the prince looked at him for some time with dim and languid eyes. Seeing him restless, Lasne asked him how he was, and whether he needed anything. He murmured, "Who knows whether my sister heard this heavenly music! It would have done her so much good to hear it!" Then the gaze of the dying child moved suddenly toward the window. A cry of joy came from his lips and, addressing the guard, he said, "I have something to tell you." Lasne went to him, taking his hand. The prisoner leaned his head on the guard's chest, who tried to hear what he was saying, but in vain; all was over. God had spared the little martyr the convulsions of the death agony, and his last dying thought remained unuttered. Lasne placed his hand over the child's heart; the heart of Louis XVII had stopped beating.

These previous cases show two aspects of psychic music—as witnessed by the dying alone and as heard by witnesses at the deathbed. Because of the different ways deathbed music is recorded, we will break down our cases into the following sections: (1) deathbed visions, (2) deathbed witnesses, and (3) related to death.

Case Type 1 — Deathbed Visions

These cases reveal rather little about the actual musical content involved but often occur simultaneously with other deathbed visions. Cases of this type were recorded prominently in a paper, "Visions of the Dying," by James H. Hyslop in the *Journal* of the ASPR, October, 1918, Vol. XII, No. 10. The following four cases are taken from that lengthy but excellent study.

Case No. 144 — Recorded by Gail Hamilton

This case was reprinted by Hyslop from Gail Hamilton's book, *X Rays*, and gives not only a good example of how music is heard accompanying deathbed visions, but how a child interprets the phenomenon. No doubt the "angels" seen were the child's way of describing the figures he saw, relating them to his own religious background.

A little lad, robust, fun-loving, free, until he was eight years old, began then to fail the body and to mature in mind, until his spiritual nature seemed to have absorbed mental and physical, in development for another world. One evening, as it began to draw toward the first day of the week, half sitting, half lying in his great easy chair, he said to his eldest sister, who was watching by him, "I think this is the last night I shall spend with you." He spoke in a perfectly calm and ordinary tone. His sister, fearing that he was dying, called in her mother, but continued to stand over him and pressed her hand upon his brow. He immediately reached up his hand as though in trouble, saying, "Don't put your hand there, H———, I don't see out of my eyes as you do. You've got your hand where my sight comes in," then lying back with closed eyes, laboring hard for breath, he suddenly exclaimed, "Oh, what a beautiful sight! See those little angels."

"What are they doing?" asked the sister.

"Oh, they have hold of hands, and wreaths on their heads, and they are dancing in a circle around me. Oh, how happy they look and they are whispering to each other. One of them says I have been a good little boy and they would like to have me come with them." He lay still awhile and then, seemingly delighted, exclaimed, "See there come some older angels—two at one end and two at the other."

"Do you know any of them?"

"Yes, Uncle E. [who died about six months before] but there are a whole row of older ones now standing behind the little ones."

"Do they say anything to you?"

"*Yes, but I can't tell you as they tell me, for they sing it beautifully. We can't sing so.*"

The child then said that the "angels" were saying that, if he were not to get better, they were going to take him with them to a new world. The little boy then saw a spirit he named "Sally," and said she was his aunt. The significant point of the case is that Sally had been dead for thirty years, and the child never knew anything of her. The child lingered on but died three months later.

Case No. 145 — Recorded by E. W. Barnett

This account was sent directly to Hyslop by the percipient's brother, E. W. Barnett, who witnessed the incident. This case is rather irregular, since the percipient recovered.

> . . . It was in the spring of 1880, I think. My brother, who was a boy of about 15 years old, had an attack of pneumonia and the attending doctor (who is now dead) told me and the other members of the family that he could not get well and that on a certain night, after he had been sick for about ten days, that he thought my brother would die. My brother had been unconscious for two or three days, so on that night that the doctor was expecting him to die, one of our neighbors and myself kept watch by his bedside. He had not spoken or showed any sign of life for more than 24 hours—and at midnight he roused up and opened his eyes and asked us to *listen to that sweet music*—he repeated it several times, saying *it was the prettiest music he ever heard and asked us if we did not hear it.* Our neighbor said to me that he was dying and I thought so too. Our neighbor said to my brother, calling him by name, "Arden, you are going to a world worth ten thousand such worlds as this." After he had spoken several times about hearing the sweet music, he went to sleep and when he awoke he was much better and continued to improve until he got well—he is living today—but he has never remembered anything about what he said to us that night. I believe he heard music from the look that was on his face.

69

Case No. 146 – Recorded by L. A. Davidson

This case is almost identical to Case No. 144, inasmuch as a young girl construed her deathbed visions as angels and heard them singing. Mr. Davidson wrote on the testimony of his mother, who witnessed the event:

> My sister, fourteen years of age, died of diphtheria. She suffered greatly until some time before her death (several hours, I believe), but was conscious to the last.
>
> Our younger brother, a child of three, had died five days before of the same disease. Just before her death my sister suddenly exclaimed, "See all of the angels!" On being asked where, she said the room was filled with them and then pointing, she said, "And there is Sanford [the dead brother]!" I believe she knew he had died. Soon after, she said, *"Hear them singing—how beautiful!"* and died at once without any struggle.

Case No. 147 – Recorded by Alice Caroline C.

This report was a firsthand account and was sent directly to Hyslop:

> The night before my brother died, I was up with him from a little after two until five o'clock. We knew he was seriously ill, but had no idea that the end was so near. In fact he was in bed only three days before he died. While I was with him he turned to me and asked if I saw the beautiful woman in white that stood by the window. I, thinking him delirious and not wishing to excite him, replied that I did. "Isn't she beautiful!" he exclaimed. Then later, "I think you'd better close the window. I'm afraid she is cold." . . . *He also asked if I heard the wonderful music* and spoke of seeing flowers. I went to my room at five, and at quarter past six he called me saying, "I think I can get up today and go into your room." I rose and went to him,

70

reaching him just in time to see his eyelids flutter and close.

Such accounts do appear in more current literature. In the spiritualist newspaper, *Light*, there appeared a case published in 1921 (page 312).

Case No. 148 — Anonymous

This case was reported by a resident of La Hague to Mr. Joseph Clark, who in turn sent it to *Light*.

> My whole family have always been fond of music, with the exception of my only sister, who disliked it. She died at about fifteen years of age, and in the very moment of her passing over she said, "I hear such beautiful music." I think the case is not only remarkable because she heard music, but because she found the music at that moment beautiful.

Case No. 149 — "John Bradley"

Cases of deathbed experiences are certainly not printed only in psychic literature. The following case, written by an attending physician, was printed in the May, 1959, issue of *Reader's Digest*. The case apparently was a pseudo-death, wherein an OOBE occurs close to death but the patient recovers. In the case, the patient John Bradley (pseudonym) died soon after the momentary recovery. The account was submitted by the attending physician, Martin C. Sampson.

The patient was in an iron lung when he seemed to expire. After an Adrenalin dose was injected into his heart and artificial respiration was attempted, he recovered. In response to the queries from the doctor on what he experienced, Bradley said:

> My pain was gone, and I couldn't feel my body. *I heard the most peaceful music.* . . . God was there and

I was floating away. The music was all around me. I knew I was dead, but I wasn't afraid. Then the music stopped, and you were leaning over me.

The patient refused to believe his experience was a dream. Death occurred shortly after.

Case No. 150 — Anonymous

The last case in this category is a brief anecdote of an incident sent to me by Miss Renée Haynes, a council member of the Society for Psychical Research and currently editor of their *Journal* and *Proceedings*. Miss Haynes writes:

> One of my sons, who is in the Foreign Service, has a nanny looking after his children, since he and his wife have so many sociabilities to cope with. I saw her last week, and out of the blue she said that, when a girl of twenty or so, training as a hospital nurse, she had been at her grandmother's deathbed and had seen the old lady sit up and say, "I'm coming! *What lovely music!*"

Case Type 2 — Deathbed Witnesses

The preceding cases all present the same difficulty. Being the experiences only of the dying themselves, could not their experiences be due to delirium? As the accounts reveal, most of the dying were in a clear state of consciousness at the time of their deaths, and there is little reason to believe they would be subject to hallucination. In fact, Karlis Osis, in his modern study of the subject, *Deathbed Observations by Physicians and Nurses*, demonstrates that many of the dying who had visions were in a clear state of awareness, with no disease or drug that could account for the visions. Nonetheless, it would be hard to convince the skeptic that these patients actually did perceive something certainly "real" though extra-mundane. To strengthen the evidence, we now record cases where the witnesses at the deathbed hear psychic music, not just the dying. In some instances this music has been heard collectively by all the death-bed witnesses, sometimes only by a part of them.

The following is a typical representation of this type of case.

Case No. 151 — F. H. Rooke

Mr. Rooke sent this case to *Light*, and it appeared in 1921 on page 321:

> Some years ago my sister and I had a joint experience which has been the greatest comfort to us.
>
> Our mother lay dangerously ill, every nerve racked with rheumatoid arthritis, and both nurse and doctor seemed to think that her sufferings could not last much longer.
>
> One night about 1 a.m. my sister was sitting up with the nurse (I was sleeping on another landing), *when her attention was transfixed by the most beautiful majestic chords, as if every golden note of melody was being played on some heavenly instrument—music far exceeding anything she had ever heard.* Turning to the nurse, she said, "Did you hear that?"
>
> "I heard nothing," was the answer.
>
> At that moment I entered the room saying, *"Where does that beautiful music come from?"* The music had awakened me out of heavy slumber.
>
> *As we spoke, the sounds died away* and, on looking at the bed, it was evident to me that the sweet spirit of our devoted mother had passed to other realms to these beautiful strains. Our father, who slept on the same floor as the invalid, and who, we felt, was entitled to hear the music, heard nothing.

This case poses certain problems about the mechanisms of the phenomenon. Clearly, inasmuch as only two of the four witnesses heard the music, the harmonies were not "objective" as we normally regard "real" sounds. This problem will be discussed in Chapter 4.

73

A rather complete account of transcendental music was given by Professor Arthur Lowell in *Light* (1912, page 324).

Case No. 152 — Professor Lowell's Pupil

My father died three weeks ago. This sad event was accompanied by a mysterious incident which I think might interest you. Perhaps it is a common occurrence, but I myself have never heard of it.

Three months before his end, he had a stroke, with loss of speech and diminution of intellectual power. He could still recognize people, though. He died one morning at dawn. I was not there, for Mama did not think she ought to call me, as there was not the slightest hope that he would regain his mental powers.

Now, here is what happened. At 2 a.m. my father entered into agony. Two minutes later (my mother had looked at the time) there began to be heard outside the window (which is on the upper story of the house) a wonderful singing which reminded my mother of a young chorister at St. Paul's Church. The voice seemed to spring from on high and to go far off into heaven like an echo of the music of paradise . . . only this time three or four voices could be distinguished singing in choir a triumphant hymn of joy. The singing went on till 2:10—that's to say for about eight minutes—then it *gradually weakened and vanished.* My father's life ended as the singing ended.

If my mother had been the only percipient, I should not have thought the incident worth repeating: one might logically have thought her state of tension made her think she heard what no human ear had ever heard. But the nurse was there too, an unusually positive and practical woman. When the music was over, she spoke to my mother (who would not have wanted to discuss with her what had taken place) saying, "Did you too hear the angels singing? I noticed it because you looked out of the window twice, much surprised. And if it wasn't angels, what else could it have been? I've heard

74

tell that angels sometimes sing at the deathbeds of very good people; but it's the first time I've ever heard the song." Such are the facts. Now it seems to me that the evidence of this woman, absolutely strange to the family, constitutes an excellent proof of the unarguable objectivity of the music perceived by my mother, whatever explanation one may posit for cleaning up the mystery. The idea that the music had a natural origin must be completely excluded to begin with. It was the middle of the night; and then our house was in an out-of-the-way place, far from all other habitations, and was surrounded by a garden beyond which stretched the countryside. Moreover, the sound of this choir did not rise from ground level, but appeared to come from just outside the window, that is to say, in midair.

Another case of music heard at a deathbed was sent to *Light* by Mrs. L. C. Gilmour (June 11, 1921). The letter was not printed, but a summary of the case was given, which I quote:

Case No. 153 — Anonymous

Writing to us on the subject of supernormal music, Mrs. L. C. Gilmour, of Brockville, Canada, relates the story of a dying man for whom his family sent to obtain the services of the parish priest. The priest was very ill, but with true heroism rose from his bed to perform the last rites at the bedside of his parishioner. After doing so, the priest collapsed and was put into a bed in the house, expiring shortly afterwards. *"During his passing the house was filled with music,* the effect being so powerful that a Protestant inmate of the place was induced to join the Roman communion."

The editors added that the correspondent herself was not Catholic and that the names of the parties involved were given.

In *NAD* we cited some examples where the music was identified as various hymns, exquisitely sung. The following case is similarly identified as one human voice:

Case No. 154 — Dr. Kenealy

The firsthand account appeared in Spicer's book, *Strange Things*, and, although the actual communication is not printed, Spicer gives his own summary of the case, based on the testimony of Dr. Kenealy at his brother's death:

> His brother's bedroom opened on a large and far-extending tract bound by green hills. In this apartment most of the members of the family—the doctor among them—were sitting about noon, the sun streaming beautifully through the thin, transparent air, *when suddenly a strain of melody more divinely sweet than any earthly music they had ever heard, rose near at hand.* It was the melancholy wail of a woman's voice, in accents betokening a depth of woe not to be described in words. *It lasted several minutes, then appeared to melt away like the ripple of the wave*—now heard, now lost in whispers till "nothing lives 'twixt it and silence." As the song commenced, the dying boy fell into the last agony, but such was the effect of the circumstances upon those who stood around that their attention was almost distracted from the solemn scene. . . . As the last note became inaudible, the child's spirit passed away.

In my survey of cases, a few similar narratives were received. Two were of this type:

Case No. 155 — Karl Artz

Mr. Artz of Elyria, Ohio, sent me a note (May 30, 1971) to the effect that when his stepmother died in 1954 he heard voices singing, "Shall We Gather at the River?" Although his sister was next to him, she heard nothing. I wrote Mr. Artz asking for more details and, if possible, a statement by his sister. In response Mr. Artz wrote:

> As to the music, it would be hard to describe, other than it was very angelic, and as they say, out of this

76

world. . . . It was very calm and peaceful and beyond that which is produced on this plane, beautiful as it might be to us, in some material.

As to masculine or feminine, or number, I would only say that it was a choral group and a blend of voices.

Mr. Artz's sister only had a vague memory that her brother had mentioned the incident to her.

Another case came from Miss E. Rinkowski (Brooklyn, New York) and gives a fairly good account of a contemporary incident, demonstrating that such cases are by no means nonexistent today.

Case No. 156 – E. Rinkowski

About three years ago my Aunt Selma passed on. She had been ill for some time with terminal cancer. Since we were all very close to her, especially me, for I was her favorite niece and she my favorite aunt, she came to live with us for some time after the doctors let her out of the hospital. She had wanted to spend her remaining time with relations she loved. The few months she had left flew by quickly as we all tried to bring into her life some remaining happiness.

One day, in early September, I felt acutely sad. Some part of me must have known that Selma would not be with us very much longer. As I brought her lunch up the stairs I felt suddenly a rush of very warm air—the type you feel in the nice days of early spring. As I stood on the landing, just a few feet from her door, *I was startled to hear faint strains of beautiful music,* that came from her room and dwelt lightly in the hall where I was. I opened the door, and I was sure then, as I am now, that Selma was seeing something that I could not, even though I did hear the music. As I stood—even more spellbound than anything else—Selma turned her head in my direction and smiled the most peaceful and happy smile I ever saw. Her head fell lightly back on the pillow, and I knew she was gone.

I can only tell you that it was the most beautiful music I have ever heard. It didn't seem to be made from any one instrument, but rather of the quality of a voice—sweet and fine—but far away. There were no words that I could hear but rather like a humming or something of that nature.

Case Type 3 — Related to Death

Psychic music not only occurs in the proximity of the dying, but is heard at a distance also. Again this adds to our evidence, for it overcomes the unlikely argument that the deathbed witnesses are in such an emotional state that they hallucinate the music.

The following reports are perhaps the strongest of all, since they definitely relate to death, but their exact nexus is unfathomable. What do these outbursts of divine harmonics mean?

Our next case is similar to deathbed cases, though the music was heard at a funeral. The account appeared in *Light*, September 24, 1921, and was taken from a story which appeared in the *Omaha World Herald:*

Case No. 157 — Mr. and Mrs. W. F. Parker

Divine music, played by celestial hands perhaps, coming from no discernible source, and filling only the room in which the body lay and the mourners sat, thrilled and awed those attendant at the funeral of the daughter of Mr. and Mrs. W. F. Parker of Wood Lake, recently.

Mr. Parker is cashier of the Citizen's State Bank of Wood Lake. Not only Mr. and Mrs. Parker, but also Ben Nickey, Wood Lake banker, Michael Flannigan, Long Pine banker, and many others who attended the funeral, which was one of the largest ever held in Cherry County, heard the heavenly strains, which welled but a short time before the final service, and sought by search and investigation to determine from whence it came. They were unsuccessful and still are at a loss for an earthly explanation. The phenomenon lasted not more than five minutes, or about as long as the rendition of an instrumental selection would require. *The faint harmonies of beautiful chords, sounding as from afar,* were first noticed by the mourners, who supposed them to be played by some organist in another room.

Gradually they grew in volume and swelled and throbbed until they filled the room, the measured rhythm of a definite theme.

Then they died away again, softening and diminishing until they seemed only an echo of a memory, and then they ceased. The mourners waited several minutes for the remainder of the service before they realized that the player was no one then in or around the house of sorrow.

The reporter adds that after strict search of the premises those present satisfied themselves that there was no earthly explanation for the music.

I think this is a very important case, since it did originally appear *outside* of psychic literature. Note that the music was heard in exactly the same manner as the cases we have extracted from psychical and spiritualist sources. Because of this independence, it adds to the growing evidence that these regularities within the reports are of great significance.

Case No. 158 — Samuel Foote

This incident, also related to a death, is of a somewhat different nature since the music occurred in coincidence with a death several miles away. The account appeared in Foote's *Memoires.* The incident is dated 1740, when Foote related having been kept awake by the "softest and sweetest strains of music" he had ever heard. Later it was discovered that the brief concert transpired at the same moment that one of his uncles, John Goodere, was having another uncle killed. Foote felt the two incidents were related.

Our final example of music which related to a death is perhaps the strangest of all, since the music was heard recurrently. The percipient of the case, whose long narrative we quote in full, was John Henry von Thünen, who was born in 1783 and lived well into the next century. The percipient was an agriculturist of note, who authored several books on his field. The account we have was not written for publication but as a letter to a friend, Christian von Buttel, describing the loss of his favorite son, Alexander, who died in 1831. The letter was later published in a German newspaper, from which it was printed in the February, 1899, issue of the German journal *Psychische Studien*. The present version is taken from the *Journal* of the S.P.R. (June, 1899), translated by Edward T. Bennett.

Case No. 159 – John Henry von Thünen

In the night between the 10th and 11th of October, three days after Alexander's death, my wife and I were awake between two and three o'clock. My wife asked me if I did not hear the distinct sound of a bell. I listened and heard such a sound, but put it down to a delusion of the senses. The following night we were again awake at the same hour, and heard the same sounds, but more clearly and distinctly. We both compared them to the striking of a bell *which was deficient in melody, but in the reverberation of which there is music*. We listened long. I asked my wife to point out the direction from which the music seemed to come, and when she indicated exactly the same spot from which I seemed to hear it, it almost took my breath away. My two sons, in spite of all their efforts, heard nothing. The same thing was repeated during the following nights. A few days later I heard the music in the evening, but it died away towards midnight, beginning again soon after 2 o'clock in the morning. On October 8th, Alexander's birthday, the music was particularly beautiful and harmonious. My wife found it extremely soothing and strengthening. But to me the feeling of rest which it produced was only transient. The uncertainty whether it was a reality or only a delusion of the senses continually disturbed me, and the endeavor to arrive at a conclusion kept me in a constant state of strain. For more than four weeks my sleep at night was so broken that I became quite worn out. I used carefully to listen if I could detect any connection between the beating of my pulse and the time of the music, but could find none. In the course of these four weeks the character of the music greatly changed; it became much stronger, so that it was audible in the midst of all kinds of noises, and was a hindrance to my reading and writing in the evening. But as it grew stronger the beautiful harmony diminished, and at this time we could only compare it to the sound produced by a number of bells clanging simultaneously. At last my wife wished it would cease, as the clanging shook our nerves and greatly affected them. In the middle of November entire peace ensued, neither my wife nor myself hearing the least sound.

Now the doubt again arose whether this music of the spheres had not been only the result of our excited state of mind and feeling. My wife felt sad and melancholy. But again after about eight days the music began, very gently at first, and continued until Christmas. On Christmas Eve it sounded, with unusual strength, clear and melodious, and with a force and variety of expression we had never before experienced. After Christmas it again ceased. On New Year's Eve we listened in vain, and this silence continued through most of January. My wife and I had now heard the music, both when we were cheerful and when we were depressed, both when we were ill and when we were well. It always came in the same manner, and apparently from the same direction. It was not possible for us any longer to entertain a doubt as to its reality. At this time we thought it had entirely departed. However, at the end of January it began again, but entirely changed in character. The sounds of bells had gone, and tones of flutes

81

took their place. At the beginning of March the music was remarkably loud and harmonious, but the tones of the flute had now vanished again, and *we could only compare it to the singing of a choir with musical accompaniment.* At one time, we both thought—though only for a moment—that we could distinguish words. On March 21st, my wife's birthday, the music assumed once more a different character, beautiful, but at the same time almost fearful. *We were neither of us able to compare it with anything earthly.*

A biography of von Thünen adds the following details about the unearthly concert:

> The wonderful music was often heard subsequently, especially on family anniversaries. It did not cease, even after the death of his wife, but continued as a faithful and loving companion through the lives of both Herr and Frau von Thünen. They admitted that these sounds, which were undeniably perceived by their ears, gave them no information as to that which was separated from them by time and space, that their intelligence and ideas were in no way extended; but believed that "your son Alexander is yet alive" was then declared to them and this firm conviction was to them their greatest joy.

No more beautiful account could be used to close this Index of Cases.

As Tyrrell said in his *The Nature of Human Personality:*

> Matter in molar masses lends itself to the illusion of discontinuity and self-completeness, which are a necessity for the simple mind of man; and the way in which his mind and senses were evolved force this illusion upon him with tremendous power. Even when the human intellect begins to form, these basic features of adaptation condition the growing mind. That is why there is a universal tendency to dismiss as rubbish evi-

dence for anything at variance with what the senses reveal—When this situation is realized, we begin to see where the real boundary of our world lies. It is not in the abyss of space, nor can either theory of space-time reveal it, nor is it to be found in the ultra-microscopical world of protons and electrons. There is no boundary existent in the Universe. All is continuous *ad infinitum;* but the way we are ourselves constructed limits what we perceive and forces upon us the necessary illusion that we perceive the whole.[11]

It is cases such as these that help us glance a bit into the outer boundaries of our universe—the mystery that is death.

---

[11] London: George Allen & Unwin, 1954, p. 69.

Part III

Chapter 3

Some Considerations of the Phenomenon

As with any case of psychic phenomena the first important consideration is whether the phenomenon can be explained normally before evaluating its paranormal qualities. In cases of deathbed music the problem is easier, since collective cases exist. But what of those subjective experiences of the dying, and of persons in normal states or during the out-of-the-body experience? These are much harder groups of experiences to analyze.

Historically, such cases have never been eagerly accepted as genuine by parapsychologists. Frank Podmore, among the first scholars to work with the Society for Psychical Research (founded in 1882), was one of the three authors of *Phantasms of the Living*. His attitude about psychic music can be found in his volume *Modern Spiritualism:*

> In dealing with clairaudience, the hearing of voices, music, and the like, we do not find any such wealth of material to assist our analysis; nor indeed does the subject lend itself so readily to systematic investigation. But there is no reason to doubt that the phenomena have,

physiologically, the same origin as the visions which we have just been considering . . . simply the result of the exaggerated activity of lower cerebral strata, released for the time from the repressive control habitually exercised by the higher centres.

René Sudre, the French psychist, has gone a step further and described such cases as perhaps due to "pathological hallucination" (*Treatise on Parapsychology*, London: Allen & Unwin, 1960).

No matter what one thinks of the above explanation, the hallucination theory must be considered and not merely brushed aside. In the previous chapter I quoted Dr. Jule Eisenbud who, tongue in cheek, remarked that the descriptions of many of the percipients seemed like the reports of patients having electrodes connected to the hypothalamus and cerebral cortex. What really must be discussed is, firstly, can there be found a neurological basis for some type of musical phenomenon? Secondly, does it seem similar to our data? And lastly, can it, in fact, explain our data?

To the first question we must answer yes. A neurological basis for hearing music was discovered by Dr. Wilder Penfield, director of the Montreal Neurological Institute. In 1955 Penfield reported on his experiments placing electrodes on the temporal lobe cortex. To quote from his report:

> The patient might exclaim in sudden surprise that he heard music, or that he heard a well-known person speaking, or that he saw something he had seen before, or that he was himself taking part in a former experience in which he was himself an actor.
>
> A young woman heard music when a certain point in the superior surfaces of the temporal cortex was stimulated. She said she heard an orchestra playing a song. The same song was forced into her consciousness over and over again by restimulation of the same spot. It progressed from verse to chorus at what must have been

the tempo of the orchestra when she had heard it playing thus. She was quite sure each time that someone had turned on a gramophone in the operating room. . . .

There were many other examples of hearing music, but always the patient heard a singing voice, or a piano, or an organ, or an orchestra, and sometimes he seemed to be present in the room or in church where he had heard it. What he heard in experience was a single occasion recalled to him with a vividness that was much greater than anything he could summon voluntarily by efforts of will.

Could this be the source of the enigmatic NAD?

Actually, Penfield's discovery has little in common with transcendental music. These differences can be categorized point by point.

1. One of Penfield's subjects felt sure that someone had turned on a radio or phonograph. Rarely in our cases of subjectively heard music did any of the percipients have the slightest doubt that they were hearing something that was beyond normal music. On rare occasions, at the *onset* of the experience, such a notion was pondered briefly, but immediately rejected.

Case No. 115 — Jeanne Hovanitz

Mrs. Hovanitz sent in her experience with psychic music to Dr. Thelma Moss of the U.C.L.A. Neuropsychiatric Institute, who referred the letter to me.

One morning, about four years ago, I was standing at the sink, doing the dishes. I was completely relaxed, looking out the window at the horses on the hill, thinking what a lovely day it was, and how nice it was with the family out to school and work, so restful. Gradually I became aware of some music in the air. It seemed to come from down the hall in the bedroom area. It became louder, and my first thought was that my teen-age daughter had left her radio on, though the music was

89

not the type of station she preferred, being symphonic rather than rock and roll. I went down to her room but discovered her radio was off. I checked all the radios in the house, all were off—*in the meanwhile the music became louder, very beautiful, sounding like a large symphony orchestra, yet there was no special tune, no theme, nothing you could hum, or follow.* There were no instruments I could identify—violin, harp, etc.—it just all blended together. I was not frightened, but went back to my dishwashing, and gradually, about five minutes later *it dissipated, just as it had begun, slowly and softly.* It left me feeling very happy, good all over, and wishing I could share this feeling and sound with everyone. Then I started questioning the validity of the whole thing—it wasn't logical—it didn't make sense. I decided not to mention it to anyone, for fear of being ridiculed. I was not in trance. . . . I was completely aware of the dishes, the soap, the house.

Mrs. Hovanitz goes on to say that she didn't feel she had some profound religious experience that altered her life . . . it was just a delightful experience.

2. Penfield emphasized in his report that his subjects heard music which was recalled from earlier experiences. As Penfield states in conclusion:

> In summary, it may be said that the electrode, applied to the temporal cortex, recalls specific occasions or events so that the individual is made aware of everything to which he was paying attention during a specific interval of time.

These experiences are not creative ones. They are merely cerebral replays of past experiences. Penfield himself compared the phenomena to the replaying of a wire recorder or film strip with sound track. NAD, on the other hand, is a creative experience. Only in extremely rare instances is the music recognized as something already experienced. In Penfield's account we find reports such as the music "progressed from verse to chorus" or of hearing a "piano." These types of experience are completely foreign to the rich supernormal data of transcendental music.

Having overcome the most serious obstacle in accepting the psi nature of NAD, the next step is to find interrelationships between the three principal forms of NAD—conscious, OOBE, and death perceptions.

In *NAD* we pointed out some highly coinciding characteristics showing the interrelation of NAD and the OOBE which, as mentioned, often includes the hearing of music. Generally, we pointed out, there are two basic similarities of the two phenomena: They both are prompted by similar mental states—absorption in nature, illness, nearness to death, being on the verge of sleep, or depression. Secondly, just as the experience is more vivid in cases of natural OOBEs (illness, or good health, and so on) and rather more vague in cases of enforced types (drowning, coercion, and so on), so music heard is vivid when catalyzed *by what would have prompted a natural projection,* and less brilliant when heard during a state which is associated with an enforced projection. This observation was dramatically supported in our analysis of OOBE cases where music was heard —*brilliant in natural cases, dull in enforced cases.* Thus, we concluded that NAD and the OOBE were interrelated.

Now, however, I wish to present a new position—that psychic music is not just *related* to the OOBE, but that transcendental music is a specific and significant characteristic *of* the OOBE.

Just what are the characteristics of the OOBE? There are several basic elements: 1. The "double" (the apparitional body that is released during astral projection) leaves via the head. 2. A blackout occurs on its release and reentry. 3. The double becomes horizontal over the body. 4. A silver cord extension is often seen. There are other lesser constituents such as clicking sounds, going through a tunnel, and so on. All these were identified and catalogued by Dr. Robert Crookall.

No better example of why I feel that psychic music is in-

91

separably related to the OOBE can be seen than in the experience of Frederic Thompson [Case No. 70], which was only very briefly discussed in *NAD*. However, the case is very important. The Thompson experience represents a case of incipient mediumship, and several examples of music are given in the huge study of the case published in the *Proceedings* of the A.S.P.R. in 1909. There are several first-hand descriptions written by Thompson in his diary. On August 3, 1907, he wrote:

> As I sketched I suddenly heard sounds of music. . . . I tried to catch some theme but could not, the music was always in changing chords and seemed to combine a great number of notes but always in harmony. After a while it died away and I did not hear it again for several days.

Thompson heard the music again on August 10th, October 19th, October 22nd, and October 23rd. One can see that in October of 1907 the music was becoming very common. These experiences led up to a magnificent vision on the 27th of October which included an out-of-the-body experience, during which the music again manifested:

> The face of the mother was transfigured with a golden light and her smile seemed to touch chords of music within me; the same chords I had heard before while sketching and this wonderful music made my happiness complete . . . in my ecstasy I clasped them in my arms. As I did so, the feeling of heavenly joy was so great that it seemed as if my soul would leave the body and it seemed as if death would be a great happiness. She then whispered to me, "The time has not yet come for you to go. . . ."

In another portion of the report, Thompson admitted having the experience of leaving the body. While the above quotation appears to be different from the OOBE, Thompson noted such significant characteristics as the feeling of ecstasy, closeness to death, the voice, the light, and a temporary paralysis—all features of the OOBE.

In October of 1007 the music became very prominent between the 19th and 27th. On the 27th, an OOBE took place. Nowhere in his diary entries does Thompson mention hearing music again. Why this sudden silence? By our theory, the music was only the incipient feature of the OOBE which finally culminated on the 27th, during which the music was, of course, again heard. Because of this I feel that the psychic music was part of the OOBE and in no way distinct from it. Why else would it have suddenly stopped after the dramatic projection?

Another observation which supports this theory comes from mediumistic literature. Mediums entering trance often report undergoing an OOBE—direct allusions can be found in the reports concerning Mrs. Leonore Piper and Mrs. Willett. By our theory, it should be expected that mediums undergoing "trance" (and thus the OOBE) should hear music. Sure enough, both Mrs. Chenoweth, the famous American medium, and Great Britain's Annie Brittain reported music when entering in, during, or on emerging from trance. This too is highly significant.

If, as we say, psychic music is but one distinct feature of the OOBE, should there be any unusual correlates with other characteristics of the OOBE? One feature often overlooked in studying the OOBE is the number of cases where a bright light is seen—sometimes at the long end of a tunnel symbolic of the departure of the "double" from the physical organism. Such a case can be exemplified in the following report taken from Ralph Shirley's *Mystery of the Human Double:* "I close my eyes and have the feeling of going over backwards . . . and I find myself going down a long dim tunnel . . . at the far end is a speck of light which grows as I approach into a large square and I am 'there' [out-of-the-body]."

Such cases are not rare, and in Crookall's collection such lights were seen in about 5 percent of the recorded cases.[1] This is a marked, though not remarkably high, percentile.

---

[1] Refer to Crookall, Case Nos. 1, 2, 15, 43, 59, 87, 118, 123, 126, 128, 168, 179, 243, 249, 254, 327, 361.

In our cases of music[2] we also noted the presence of this light, as in the following case from Crookall's collection [*NAD* Case No. 10].

> I was given ether. *I seemed to float down a dark tunnel, moving towards a half-moon of light that was miles away. I heard the sound of music* and smelled the scent as of an old-fashioned bouquet. Then my flight down the tunnel was halted: although there was no obstruction, I could not go further. I staged a rebellion. I wanted to go on. A voice said, "Go back and live." Then I found myself back in the body.

In my collected cases a light was seen accompanying the music at the rate of almost 33 percent! This is a remarkable and, in fact, staggering statistic, and much beyond what would be expected by chance which, based on Crookall's cases, would be about 5 percent. Accompanying this finding is an even more striking fact that the *color* of the light is different in OOBE cases when no music is heard and when music *is* heard.

Invariably when a color is mentioned the light is described as white.

Crookall's Case No.[3]
>1: "There came a light, a brilliant white light, blinding in its unearthly radiance."
>2: "I cannot describe that bright, yet ethereal light—intense. . . ."
>15: "Then suddenly appeared an opening like a tunnel, and at the far end a light."
>43: "I looked further. Afar off, a brilliant gleam of light burst out, flooding the road with inconceivable glory. . . ."

---

[2] Refer to Rogo, Case Nos. 3, 4, 11, 70, 77, 90, 106.

[3] All these case numbers refer to Crookall's two volumes, *The Study and Practice of Astral Projection* (Case Nos. 1–160) and *More Astral Projections* (Case Nos. 161–382).

118: "I was surrounded by a great light or white cloud which blotted out all the surroundings."

126: "I turned away from the bright light which shone on my left and entered a gloomy tunnel. I fought my way back to a tiny light in the distance."

168: "In the darkness I saw a light approaching: it was like the white screen in the 'movies.'"

243: "I . . . saw a very bright light which got bigger as it approached."

249: "I look upward where the steps merge into a brilliant white light."

254: "I was at the bottom of a chimney-like tunnel which had a patch of light showing at the top."

327: "Have you ever looked through a very long tunnel and seen the tiny speck of light at the far end? I found myself . . . along just such a tunnel."

361: "I found myself in a dark, windy tunnel . . . I could see distant lights."

While the above OOBE cases indicate that the color of the light is not frequently described, when the color is referred to, it is invariably white.

Cases of a light seen with music heard are drastically different, since a white light has rarely been reported. Instead a golden light is described when the color is mentioned at all:

Case No.[4]

4: ". . . floating up in a golden glow towards a wonderful light."

70: ". . . the face was transfigured with a golden light." (This section was not quoted in the account I gave of the case.)

77: "I wanted to walk into the sun [seen afar, presumably gold]."

Others describe it in only general terms as "a brilliant light" [Case No. 3], "a faraway brightness" [Case No. 11], a "vision of

---

[4] These numbers refer to cases cited in my previous volume *NAD* and in the present book.

95

a light" [Case No. 90], "kaleidoscopic glow of light" [Case No. 105], and "a bright light" [Case No. 106]. Again the *color* of the light is not often recorded but, when it is, invariably it is gold— a feature extremely rare in cases where music was *not* heard. (In all of Crookall's records only his Case No. 179 describes a golden light.)

To recapitulate: Lights are seen in much higher numbers during OOBEs wherein music is heard. Secondly, just as the color of the light is described as white in regular OOBEs, it is reported as gold in musical OOBEs.

The critical point which is to be made appears to be that the NAD, although we have proven it has a definite relation to the OOBE, not only appears with it, but appears in conjunction with specific characteristics of the OOBE. Because of this, we reaffirm our belief that transcendental music is but another characteristic of the OOBE and is in no way independent of it, even when the relationship is vague.

A third area of congruity can be made between the way in which the OOBE takes place and the way psychic music is perceived in normal states and at deathbeds.

The "double" does not leave the physical body in one stage, but in two stages, according to Dr. Crookall in his *Out-of-the-Body Experience: A Fourth Analysis* (New Hyde Park, N.Y.: University Books, 1970). Crookall's mass data reveal that uniting the physical body and the "double" is a dense, shell-like "vehicle of vitality" which acts as a cohesive between the two bodies and is the force capable of producing telekinesis and various other physical phenomena of mediumship. Stage one of the OOBE is quitting the physical body, and stage two consists of the release from the vehicle of vitality. Upon re-entering the organism, the "double" rejoins first the vehicle of vitality and then the physical body in a two-stage return.

Crookall based his theory on his own studies of hundreds of reports. In many of these he noted that after the initial release of the double the percipients made remarks such as being enveloped in "a foggish light" or "fog," experiencing a "stifled and cramped feeling," and the tunnel effect we have discussed. These doubles then lay horizontal above the physical body (this position is found in 23.3 percent of natural OOBEs and 18.9 percent of enforced projections).

In the second stage these same reporters made such statements as "increasing light," "the mists disappeared . . . bright light." Mrs. Piper, the great American medium who was studied for almost half a century by the Society for Psychical Research and the American Society for Psychical Research, describes an OOBE as though she passed through "a dark veil." Then "everything looked so bright" (Ref. *Proceedings* S.P.R., 1911). Mrs. Piper's remarks illustrate some sort of two-stage process during astral projection. The "doubles" were then released from their horizontal position and became erect.

Upon reentering the physical body, our narrators report experiences of "entering a gloomy tunnel," or a "return journey through a mist." The "doubles" again returned to the horizontal position (somewhat rarer in the case studies, appearing only 3.2 percent of the time in natural OOBEs).

The second stage is the return through the tunnel, just as emerging from it is indicative of the release.

Before the publication of Crookall's book I had stumbled onto a similar phenomenon with NAD—discovering that psychic music is in two stages—gradually being heard, rising to full power, and receding again. This is the "crescendo" effect, which we noted in our first study but did not interpret at that time. Just as the double is released into a gloomy world of the "vehicle of vitality" and then into clarity, so psychic music initially manifests quietly and in the distance, rapidly crescendos to full volume, and then disappears gradually. From our cases we find: "At first the music was barely heard but it steadily gained in volume until it was clearly and distinctly heard, and it then diminished until it faded out completely" [Case No. 1]. "First the music was soft and to the right of me, then louder, much louder. . . . It came from farther and farther, and higher and higher until it died away" [Case No. 17]. "I became conscious

97

of a deep murmuring sound . . . yet the sound increased . . . a mighty chorus swept down over the hills . . . [and] gradually dispersed into silence" [Case No. 19].

Sometimes the two stages of the music are more apparent. First it may manifest as a bird singing or chirping, and then the music suddenly bursts out. Mrs. A. C. F. [Case No. 34] records, ". . . a single bird started to chirp in the darkness outside the window. We both left our chairs and went to look out. We could see nothing . . . the room was suddenly filled with the sound of an organ playing and voices singing a hymn." Compare this two-stage manifestation with the report of the mystic Orsola Benincasa [Case No. 86], where nuns reported, "At such times [in ecstasy] musical sounds which some described as like the song of a bird seemed to come from her breast. She did not sing but they heard a ravishing harmony which could only have a supernatural origin." And finally, D. D. Home reports on the death of his wife [Case No. 110], "Distant musical sounds were heard . . . and on more than one occasion the singing of a bird. . . ." These cases, too, exemplify the two-stage process of the music.

However, not all music is heard in two stages, just as many OOBE accounts seem to have only a one-stage release: a projection into clearness, a momentary blackout, and then a reentry. Our music cases show the sudden outburst of music quickly fading away. Peggy Mason reports [Case No. 25], "I heard a great burst of what I can only call 'celestial music.' It seemed like a burst of joy, lasting a few seconds, then fading away." See also Case No. 42.

Our interpretation of this unique parallel is that the crescendo of the music corresponds to the loosening of the "double," still enshrouded by the "vehicle of vitality." On being released from the "vehicle of vitality" the music is heard in full volume and then diminishes as the process reverses itself. An out-of-the-body experience manifests when these bodies separate. In our cases occurring in normal states and at deathbeds, it represents not necessarily a "release" but a loosening, even though a full OOBE did not take place.

We can validate this interpretation by examining music heard during OOBEs. We see that in these cases we do find accounts of a double-stage manifestation of the music, corresponding to the double-stage OOBE. We find reports of: "To my ears came a beautiful sine wave note . . . which increased from zero to a volume which seemed to fill the universe" [Case No. 6]. "I left my body and went straight up [the 'releasing' of the bodies] but all the time I could hear music and the higher I got the louder the music became" [Case No. 7]. "The music swelled in intensity and seemed to ebb" [Case No. 14]. All these reports were *during* OOBEs and parallel NAD heard in normal states.

The reader may have noted that some of these extracts are similar to deathbed cases which were heard collectively. This seems odd, since projection cases appear to be subjective, as do cases in normal states of consciousness. (See Case No. 1, where Raymond Bayless heard the music while in a room with another individual who remained deaf to it.) Why this irregularity? We shall delve into this mystery in our chapter on how pyschic music is "heard."

This fairly well sums up the vast coincidentals between NAD and the OOBE. Let us make a point-by-point summary of our data showing the parallels.

1. The OOBE and NAD manifest during similar mental states.

2. Just as music is heard vividly in conditions that would produce a natural OOBE, so the music is dull during mental states conducive to enforced OOBEs. Likewise, natural OOBEs are more vivid in experiences than enforced ones.

3. Music heard *during* OOBEs is more vivid in natural cases than enforced ones.

4. Music is heard in normal states *just as often* as during the OOBE.

Now, the points which indicate that the music is actually a *characteristic* of the OOBE and not an independent phenomenon:

1. Music has been noted to lead up to an OOBE and manifest during it.

2. An orb of light, usually white, is reported during some

99

OOBEs. This light is noted in a far higher percentage of cases where music is also heard. In these cases the light tends to be gold. These features show that music appears to manifest in conjunction with certain *other* characteristics of the OOBE.

3. Just as many OOBEs have a two-stage release, so music is heard in two stages. These stages sometimes recur at the end of the experience.

4. Music heard *during* OOBEs have this same feature.

All these sets of data lead us to postulate that music is only indicative of an OOBE, either actually taking place, or an incipient projection. This is not to say that NAD *is* the OOBE, but that psychic music is not an experience of our physical organism as is, for example, telekinesis, but of the "double" which can almost never be experienced unless an OOBE is in process. We are now left to determine the relationships between the OOBE and the death experience, showing why deathbed music is heard and how it relates to the above data.

In order to explain psychic music heard at deathbed by our theory that the music is a function of the OOBE, we must postulate that the death experience is, in fact, the same as the OOBE. In the death situation, though, the projection is permanent. This is in no way difficult . . . Sir William Barrett noted that clairvoyants at deathbeds witnessed the release of the "double" at death. The most interesting aspect of these cases is their remarkable congruity, since they were recorded by many individuals in different times and places, yet all described a similar phenomenon:

1. Florence Marryat, the Victorian authoress, wrote in her volume *The Spirit World* (1894) that upon witnessing a sister's death a narrator saw something "like a cloud of smoke," which gathered above her head and acquired the shape of the girl's body." It was "suspended in air, two or three feet above the body, 'bound by' cords of light like electricity." She also saw apparitions about the body.

2. G. Maurice Elliott, an Anglican minister, often administered

to the dying and many times witnessed the "soul" leaving the body. One such observation was shared by his wife and is recorded in his *Angels Seen Today* (1919): "We saw, just above the bed a white hazy mist. . . . In a very short while it took the perfect form of the suffering one . . . a silvery cord was attached to the physical soul body and helpers severed this."

3. A third case is written by W. Tudor-Pole in his anonymously published book *Private Dowding* (1919): "Directly above the dying man I see a shadowy form that hovers in a horizontal position, about two feet above the bed. The form is attached to the physical body by two transparent cords . . . the figure grows until it is a counterpart of the body." Tudor-Pole also saw figures sever the cord.

In this same vein we can quote from Ernesto Bozzano, the Italian psychist, citing a missionary from Tahiti who reported to him the native "superstition" that "shortly after a human body ceases to breathe, a vapour rises from its head, hovering a little way above it, but attached by a vapoury cord. This vapour gradually increases in bulk and assumes the form of the inert body. When this becomes quite cold, the connecting cord disappears and the disentangled soul-form floats away as if borne by invisible couriers" [*The Metaphysical Magazine*, October, 1896].

These cases are all perfect allusions to the OOBE experience. We have already noted the horizontal position of the released "double" over the physical body. In Crookall's studies there are over fifty allusions to this.[5] We find such characteristic statements as, "I always began lying horizontally over my body, floating outwards" [Case No. 86]; "I rose horizontally above it (the physical body)" [Case No. 68]; or "I then became aware of being parallel to my body, some two or three feet above it" [Case No. 301].

---

[5] See Crookall's *More Astral Projections*, page 143, List E, for exact references.

The next parallel is the mention of the cord which attaches the double to the physical body, usually at the head. Again, this common feature is experienced in about 20 percent of natural cases and 16.2 percent in enforced projections.[6] Here we find coincidental statements such as: "A small cord like a spider's web" [Case No. 3]; "My two identical bodies were joined by means of an elasticlike cable" [Case No. 20]; "I saw a shining white cord, two or three inches wide . . . stretching from my body" [Case No. 91]; and so on.

Finally, these people saw "helpers" release the double. This feature is noted in several cases also. Many projectors report either seeing the dead or, in many instances, noting that apparitions helped them to separate from the physical body.[7] In fact, this characteristic is so interesting that Crookall has devoted an entire book, *During Sleep,* to its study.

As is well known, *the* most common deathbed vision is the seeing of figures or apparitions of the dead. Often these figures represent a relative or friend whom the dying person had no way of knowing had died. Such cases were studied extensively by William Barrett and also by the American researcher, James H. Hyslop. Currently Dr. Karlis Osis has made a study of such manifestations and has issued his findings in *Deathbed Observations by Physicians and Nurses* (New York: Parapsychology Foundation, 1961).

One such case—a rather famous one—was originally collected by Minot Savage, an American clergyman, and has found its way into virtually every study of deathbed visions. The case concerns two children, both suffering from diphtheria in June, 1889. Jennie died first on a Wednesday. Her sick playmate, Edith, was not told of her friend's death. On Saturday Edith was dying, and she said, "Why, papa, I am going to take Jennie with me! Why, papa! You did not tell me that Jennie was here! Oh Jennie, I am so glad you are here!" She died soon afterward.

---

[6] *Ibid.,* List L.

[7] *Ibid.,* List I.

In many cases the dying person realizes that the figures have come to take them away into death and the after-life. These cases indicate that, just as clairvoyants at deathbeds see "helpers," the dying themselves are quite aware of their presence.

All these data have a critical bearing on our case studies of NAD. Obviously, since the dying are undergoing a permanent form of the OOBE, they should often hear music. Notice, however, in our own cases of this type (subjective experiences of the dying, Case Nos. 36, 37, 38, 94, 95, 96) while music was heard, *none of the percipients heard the music fade away.* This is quite in keeping with our theory, since the decrescendo of the music occurs when the "double" reunites with the physical body. At death no reunion takes place, and we should expect that the music would not fade out—and this is shown in our collected cases! There are also instances where the music was heard during a deathbed vision. Such cases are on record. For instance, Sissy [Case No. 96] reported: "The music is strangely enchanting —Oh! here is Sadie, she is with me [Sadie was her little girl who had died ten years before]."

Why then do deathbed visitors also hear the music? The key is in the fact that clairvoyants at deathbeds have heard the music *and* seen the soul leaving the body.

Case No. 116 — J. Willis Ring

This case is taken from the journal, *The Forum of Psychic and Scientific Research* (December, 1933). Ring witnessed the death of his mother:

> As I sank in a chair nearby, I observed a vapor somewhat resembling steam, rising from my mother's body . . . soon there appeared, beside my mother, her two mothers. [She had been adopted as a child.] With gentle passes they drew forth . . . her spiritual body. . . . The light of their presence and the *soothing music* which attended them relieved the despair of the scene. . . . Soon I heard the "click." The "thread snapped."

The reader can now grasp the total interrelationships between music heard at deathbeds, during OOBEs, and in normal consciousness. Just because a percipient does not leave his body in an OOBE does not mean, as our data suggest, an incipient projection is not occurring. Persons at deathbeds, although they do not see the release of the "double," still may hear the music accompanying the final OOBE.

This all leaves but one more problem to fathom. Why is deathbed music sometimes collectively perceived, while music heard during OOBEs and natural projection cases is subjective? As we noted, the descriptions of the phenomenon are just about identical. How can the same phenomenon manifest in both a seemingly objective *and* also a subjective form? And how does this affect our theory of the interrelationships of the music? To this seeming Gordian knot we now turn.

Chapter 4

Psychic Music: Sense Perception or Psychic Perception?

Our first volume, NAD, like Phantasms of the Living, Barrett's Deathbed Visions, and the Census of Hallucinations, was basically only an attempt to gather as much evidence as possible for the phenomenon under consideration, and was not devoted to an in-depth theoretical discussion. One specific problem encountered with deathbed music as, to a lesser degree, with all psychic music, is whether it is perceived through normal sensory means ("hearing") or by a more complex psychic system akin to, but not the same as, clairaudience. Hitherto I used the age-old argument that the case was objective (and like any sound of the "real" world) similar to the objectivity of apparitions—that, since the music is sometimes heard collectively, the phenomenon is implied to be physical or objective. However, in light of reconsideration I feel that there is sufficient evidence which would necessitate the belief that all psychic music, even when collectively witnessed, is not heard by normal sense perception, and that the theory of "collective psychic hallucination" as an explanatory model is not as improbable as it may seem.

In our studies, several collectively heard cases were quoted, such as that of Mrs. Sewell's daughter [Case No. 31] in which sounds of "an Aeolian harp" were heard by Mrs. Sewell and several servants. Mrs. A. C. F's case [No. 34] stated that both she and her brother-in-law heard psychic music. In his report to the Dialectical Society, H. D. Jencken [Case No. 35] told of a case of music heard by a nurse and the servants. (Also see Case No. 43 for a similar instance heard by several witnesses.)

Obviously these cases *seem* to imply that the music was heard by normal sensory channels. However, any judgment as to whether or not normal sensory functions would explain the phenomenon would have to be founded on two basic qualities of human perception: (1) that everyone perceives the same thing when the stimulus originates from a common source, and (2) that the organs of perception (eyes, ears, *et cetera*) are not obstructed in any way.

It was with considerable surprise that I realized psychic music violates both these basic principles!

As for the first breach of the principles of perception we cited, collectively heard music is not necessarily perceived in the same manner by all the witnesses. Indeed, the music was *heard* collectively, but not *perceived* collectively. No better example can be found than in the case of Mrs. L. [Case No. 32] which was originally published in *Phantasms of the Living*, Volume 11, which was only briefly described in *NAD*. I had not then realized the importance of the case. There were several witnesses at the deathbed of Mrs. L: Mrs. H., Dr. G., Mrs. I., Eliza W., and Charlotte C. The original memorandums were sent to Edmund Gurney, principal author of *Phantasms*. Mrs. I. heard the music as "low, soft music, exceedingly sweet, and of three girls' voices." Mr. L., the husband of the dying woman, heard nothing at all. Dr. G. heard the music as "not unlike that of an Aeolian harp." At the same time, Eliza W. could distinguish the words, "The strife is o'er, the battle done."[1]

---

[1] This is similar to Lord Adare's account of music heard in the presence of D. D. Home [Case No. 67]. Adare heard only organlike music, while Home could distinguish words.

It is clear that in this case we have three orders of hearing. The most complex is the hearing of singing with words; the next singing alone; and then harplike music. For good measure we can add on Mr. L., who heard nothing. It is not mentioned whether or not Mr. L. had any hearing defect, but we would assume he did not.

This case transgresses many factors of normal sense perception. Although various individuals hear at different levels of acuteness, the odds are quite against its being a natural occurrence that *all* the witnesses at Mrs. L.'s deathbed heard the music in different terms. And although it is well known in standard psychological literature that individuals have a wide variance in how they perceive, interpret, and misinterpret vague sounds and articulations, nothing can compare with the *specific* levels encountered in the above instance.

The case of John Britton also supports the theory that psychic music is not heard by sense perception. The phenomenon, originally reported in the *Journal* of the S.P.R., Volume IV, page 181, was clearly heard collectively by John Britton and various relatives. *The unique feature of the case was that Britton was a deaf mute, but still heard the music!*

Case No. 117 — John Britton

The narrator of the case was S. Allen, Britton's brother-in-law. Both he and his wife heard music coming from upstairs and rushed up to Britton's room:

> We found Jack lying on his back with his eyes fixed on the ceiling, and his face lighted up with the brightest of smiles. After a little while Jack awoke and used the words "heaven" and "beautiful" as well as you could by means of his lips and facial expressions. As he became more conscious, he also told us in the same manner that his brother Tom and his sister Harriet were coming to see him. This we considered very unlikely as they lived some distance off, but shortly afterwards a cab drove up

from which they alighted . . . after Jack's partial recovery, when he was able to write or converse upon his fingers, he told us that he had been allowed to see into heaven [an OOBE?] and *to hear most beautiful music.*

The Reverend L. S. Milford, who interviewed the Allens, wrote:

> Mrs. Allen says the sounds she heard resembled singing—sweet music without distinguishable words—that she went upstairs directly she heard the music which continued until she reached the bedroom. Mr. Allen's impression is that the sounds resembled the full notes of an Aeolian harp.

Note here the double level of the music: Mrs. Allen hearing singing while Mr. Allen presumably heard instrumental sounds.

The case dramatically demonstrates that the music is not dependent on normal sense perception. In fact, the case creates a double enigma. Not only is it unique for cases of deathbed music (often heard by the dying person only and, reversely, heard collectively by everyone *except* the patient [see Case No. 31]), but in the whole realm of psychism as well. Although, for example, apparitions have been seen differently by various percipients, I know of no case wherein a blind man felt the presence of an apparition—much less "saw" one!

These two cases seem to lead us to the conclusion that, if we wish to understand deathbed music, we must look further than the study of normal sense perception. Of course, one is prompted to deal with the question, "Could not psychic music be perceived in a variety of ways—sometimes through sensory response to a physical stimulus, sometimes on other occasions by a psychic perception?" At first this argument would appear logical, since in shifting our focus to the study of apparitions, certainly an apparition seen collectively and in different perspective concordant to the position of the onlookers is of a different nature than an apparition seen of a man being hanged along with the phantom of the tree in the apparitional vision.[2] However, the answer lies again in the case of Mrs. L. In reading a large body of cases, especially those involving deathbed music, we observe that the music is usually heard as singing of specific hymns, *or* harplike music, *or* a soft female choir. The case of Mrs. L. is one of the very few where there were a large number of observers present, all of whom wrote memorandums of the experience. Most cases do not give details of the number of witnesses or give in-depth descriptions of the music heard. Usually, though, it is evident that only one or two individuals heard the music. However, when the music was heard by a large group of percipients collectively in one case, all the common descriptions found individually in scattered reports are given by the different witnesses, showing, probably, that the common descriptions of the music—harplike, singing, and so on—are not due to differences in the music heard, but in the psychic perception of the different percipients.

This is the unique quality of the case of Mrs. L. Had only one or two persons been at her deathbed, perhaps both would have heard the music in the same fashion. The important point I wish to make is that the different form in which each independent onlooker heard the music corresponds to the different perceptions around the deathbed of Mrs. L. The accounts in no way differ from the pattern set by other cases, and thus I feel certain that deathbed music is always heard by one single mechanism—a psychic one—and any explanation of the music will be forthcoming as a theory that the phenomenon is nonobjective (in the sense of the "real" world) while taking into full consideration the paradox that the music is collectively perceived.

These data explain how we can state that deathbed music is allied to the OOBE (always subjective) and still explain the unusual data showing that music in these cases can be collectively heard. The problem now remaining is *why* only psychic

---

[2] See Tyrrell's *Apparitions* (Myers Memorial Lecture, 1942) or Camille Flammarion's *Death and Its Mystery* (three volumes; New York: Century Co., 1921).

music heard at deathbeds reveals this feature of collectivity, and why deathbed music is heard as singing or Aeolian harp music or something similar; while music heard in normal states and OOBEs is described as beyond earthly music with no such comparisons usually made, and, finally, why some witnesses hear the music in one way and others in a different mode. These problems will be confronted in the chapter on the actual mechanics of the phenomenon.

Chapter 5

Psychic Music: Some Unusual
Manifestations

It would seem that we have come to the point where a general theory should be offered to account for the NAD phenomenon. Elucidating patterns which control the phenomenon is a cornerstone in an attempt to discover the actual psychical mechanics of the manifestations. However, showing the interrelationships between the three principal forms of the phenomenon and how the key to their mystery lies in the OOBE does not explain the origin or actual nature of the music itself.

In considering a theory to explain psychic music, we would be less than honest if we did not offer a theory *in light of* similar phenomena which, although they appear to be the same as the type of music we have been analyzing, nevertheless do not fit into the general patterns we have been discussing. These cases, initially, do not seem to relate to the OOBE.

One of the richest sources of music phenomena can be found in haunting cases. While these usually consist of phantasmal organ playing, isolated musical sounds, and so on, there are some cases where clearly defined music was heard and as such shall be considered.

Case No. 118 — The Tweedale Haunting

Hauntings have the unfortunate habit of being poorly observed, poorly reported, remote, and poorly investigated. All these pitfalls were corrected in the haunting at Weston Vicarage, the abode of the Reverend Charles Tweedale, an Anglican minister and his wife and family. The haunting was principally recorded from 1905 to 1923 but continued well into the 1930s. Among the many witnesses was W. W. Baggally, a council member of the S.P.R., whose principal fame lies in his membership on the 1908 commission appointed by the S.P.R. to investigate Eusapia Palladino.

The sources of the reports on the phenomena, which seemed to be a composite of haunting manifestations and his wife's psychic abilities, were printed in two of Charles Tweedale's books, *Man's Survival of Death* (1909) and *News from the Next World* (1940). The phenomena, comprising one of the most active hauntings on record, included phantoms, independent voices, raps, telekinesis, and so on.[1]

One manifestation of music was heard on April 23, 1933. Tweedale records:

> Half an hour after my wife and Mr. Baggally had left the house for church, the girl Ida went upstairs to the nursery on the third floor to change her dress. While there, she heard beautiful singing coming from the Grey Room, which is at the other end of the house on the same floor. She ran downstairs with the dress in her hand to the other girl Rosetta and told her, and together they came up to the landing below the third floor and listened. Both heard the most beautiful singing coming from the Grey Room, and this continued for quite five minutes. It sounded like a hymn, though they could not distinguish the words, but the tune was that of

---

[1] Apparitions of animals were seen as well. See Raymond Bayless's *Animal Ghosts* (New Hyde Park, N.Y.: University Books, 1970).

the hymn, "Peace, Perfect Peace." Rosetta described the singing as a kind of crooning or humming very sweetly sung, but the words not distinguishable [*News from the Next World*, p. 145].

A couple of days later, Tweedale learned that his aunt had died on the evening the maids heard the music and at the precise time.

This case seems initially to resemble some of the cases collected in our first volume [that is Case Nos. 41 and 44] of music related to death. However, in this report the percipient-to-be, Tweedale himself, did not hear the music. Instead it was heard by two disinterested parties. Because of this, it is hard to classify the case as an independent phenomenon or part of the over-all haunting of the vicarage. Because the haunting was overlaid by many subsidiary events—premonitions, alleged discarnate communications, and so on—it seems this latter explanation should be the favored one.

A less dramatic manifestation of music occurred in 1909, a short time before the principal outbreak of the haunting. Tweedale reports:

> *May 31, 1909*—My wife awoke about 2 a.m. and after attending to baby Dorothy, now about a month old, lay awake a little while. As she lay awake, a strain of music began to sound from the top of the wardrobe. It was most beautiful, and the tone something like that produced by a musical box [*ibid.*, p. 37].

There was no musical box in the house at the time. Compare Tweedale's description to an anonymous haunting reported in the S.P.R. *Proceedings*, Volume VI [Case No. 53] where one of the principal witnesses, Anne H., describes music similarly, "It sounded like a musical box to me."

There were other more limited musical manifestations such as violin sounds [similar to W. Stainton Moses, Case No. 68].

The Great Welsh Revival[2]

Like the Tweedale haunting, the celestial music heard by various witnesses in South Wales at the turn of the century represented only a small part of a very complex outbreak of psychic phenomena. However, instead of being confined to a small vicarage, the psychic atmosphere which apparently ignited the phenomena swept over all of South Wales in 1904–5. Before considering the music actually heard, we should outline the basic history of what is one of the most peculiar psychical *and* psychological religious outbreaks in modern history.

The revival chiefly centered on Evan Roberts, who trained as a Calvinist Methodist minister, during which period he had a number of religious experiences. Spurred by his experiences he mounted a preaching campaign through Wales. His revival meetings began receiving serious attention and news coverage, and soon a religious mania grasped the Welsh religious community. However, it is not to be thought that the Great Welsh Revival was solely Roberts' doing, since the seeds of a revival had been germinating for some time. It seems that Roberts' uncanny charisma was the final pressure before the grand outbreak of religious hysteria.[3]

It is not odd that in times such as these many adherents of the new gospel are the victims of gross pathological delusions and hallucinations. However, it is true that cases of genuine mystical experiences and psychic experiences come to the forefront at these same times in order to (usually naïvely) give credence to the movement.

Two of the more common phenomena recorded were psychic lights and music. The source is the Reverend A. T. Fryer's

---

[2] No case number is given, since the music (again a small part of a great many manifestations) was independently witnessed throughout Wales by a number of observers, each of whom will be given a case number.

[3] Refer to Francis Younghusband's *Modern Mystics* (1935) now reissued by University Books. See also W. T. Stead's *The Revival in the West* (London, 1905). Stead covered the Welsh Revival as a journalist.

"Psychological Aspects of the Welsh Revival: 1904–5," *Proceedings:* S.P.R., Pt. LI, December, 1905.

Case No. 119 — Mrs. J. M.

This incident was reported by the Reverend H. P. J. and vouched for by the Reverend Fryer. Fryer himself interviewed the woman and received the following statement of music heard accompanying the apparitions of her dead children:

> I began to feel queer, the room went all dark, and it seemed as if the room was full, or like a swarm of bees around me. I went out to the back yard and I saw about a dozen men going into church, so I said to myself, "Why should I be against my husband doing good when others are going to be good?" Turning into the house again, [I saw] the kitchen was beautiful and light as if the sun was shining there. I went back to the wash tub and there before me appeared the four children, and one of them spoke in English to me saying, "Ma'am, come" and then they disappeared. *I could hear the singing of the hymn "O Paradiso" until it died away in the distance* [page 93, 131–33].

This case could be explained as an incipient OOBE, since the common fading away of the music is noted. There are several cases on record of music accompanying apparitions. (See Case Nos. 38, 45, 93, 96, 100.)

Case No. 120 — Cases from Montgomeryshire

These reports were sent to Fryer by a minister in Montgomeryshire and account for three separate incidents (pages 93–94, 133–34):

1. D. D., J. J., and R. J., during the service at the Parish Church, heard bells chiming on January 29th. The sound was over their heads. There were many of them, but they were the only ones that heard it.

2. E. E. on Saturday evening, between seven and eight, while returning home from his work, heard strange music similar to the vibrations caused by telegraph wires (only much louder) on an eminence, the hill being far away from any trees and wires of any kind, and it was more or less a still evening.

3. J. P. heard some lovely singing on the road, about half a mile from his home, on Saturday evening, three weeks ago, which frightened him very much.

The first incident could easily have been a hallucination, especially had one of the witnesses stated that he heard chiming, after which others often use the remark as a subject for autosuggestion. Such cases are not unique in emotion-stirred meetings. The two other cases are too brief for any comment, although *fear* is an emotion *not* associated in our accounts of psychic music, the percipient usually describing the phenomenon as a very pleasurable experience.

Of the entire report the best single incident of supernormal music comes from the vicar of a parish in Cariganshire. The report, including an interview with the percipient, is given in Fryer's paper:

Case No. 121 – A Vicar

A few days before Christmas, 1904, I was riding to see some parishioners in —— parish. They lived about three miles up the hillside. As I was gradually ascending I fancied I heard voices singing. I took little notice for the moment, believing it was pure fancy. *Gradually the voices seemed to increase in volume, until at last they became overpowering.* I was trying to imagine it could be nothing outside myself, as it were, but the wonderful harmony seemed to be borne on me entirely from the outside, and was as real to my senses as anything I have ever heard.

I could distinguish the words distinctly. [Here were inserted four lines in Welsh.]

The moment the refrain would come to an end it would be restarted, the volume becoming greater and

116

greater. To me it was an exquisite sensation. *When about arriving at my destination, the voices suddenly ceased.* I have had no trace of the recurrence of such a thing, and never had such an experience previously [pages 94, 136–37].

The vicar did not recollect ever having the verse before. This experience could have been related to an OOBE but for two exceptions: The music stopped suddenly, which is unusual, and the music was identified as a verse, common with deathbed music, rare with OOBEs or in natural states.

Case No. 122 – Mr. and Mrs. L. M.

L. M.'s report is chiefly associated with the psychic lights so dominant during the Welsh Revival. Both he and his wife saw a light like a cross in the sky joined by another, accompanied by a singing voice. Mrs. L. M. heard the music again "like a well-trained choir," along with lights. Both manifestations were witnessed by two other observers. The woman could not identify the music or the words [page 150].

That concludes our survey of the Welsh Revival. One wonders whether such cases really were related to the actual revival or whether they were independent psychical events which ordinarily would not have been recorded had it not been for the outbreak of religious frenzy flowing over South Wales. In any event the witnesses seemed, whether right or wrong, to associate the music with the revival. Such is not odd. Cases of psychic music also were recorded during France's infamous Huguenot persecutions, the Irish Revival of 1859, and in the records of the Mormons in the United States. On the other hand, it is significant that such movements prompt so many reports of psychic music.

The Welsh Revival, like the Tweedale haunting, shows that psychic music may not always be a personal or private experience. While all the occurrences we cited seem more or less to fall into one of our standard categories, there was an impersonal "psychic atmosphere," so to speak, which complicated them—whether it was a haunting or a religious revival. Because of this, these cases are presented apart from the others so that special attention may be given this impersonal factor in working out a general theory.

Chapter 6

The Music of "The Next World"?

Robert Crookall in his first book, *The Supreme Adventure* (London: James Clarke, 1961), offered a composite study of mediumistic communications—from the records of the S.P.R. to popular spiritualistic books which became much in vogue during and directly after World War I—which shows that, regardless of era or quality, "communicators" generally describe the same experiences to which they were subjected during the death experience. These patterns are cross-cultural, as I showed in *NAD* (Appendix A). It was during his work on this theme that Crookall discovered that the "dead" describe the final leaving of the body in identical terms to those having OOBEs near death (pseudodeaths). And it was this discovery that led him to his monumental study of the OOBE and its relevance to survival.

In this chapter we shall be engaged in a similar endeavor: (1) To see what "communicators" say about music heard at their deathbeds, and on music in the "next world" and (2) should this be fruitful, whether these data help ascertain any general theory to account for the phenomenon.

It should be pointed out that we are not assuming that each

119

book quoted necessarily offers a good case or that the "communications" actually are spiritistic in nature. All we are doing is logging cases—descriptions from books which *purport to be* "*communications*" from the "other side." Our law of content analysis again holds true. Will patterns occur which seem to validate these works?

It is certainly not an arbitrary decision to search spiritualistic literature for possible clues to the enigma of psychic music. Many cases of NAD seem definitely to point in that direction. If we recapitulate our cases, we find that M. E. Henley heard music while experiencing an OOBE during which she heard the voice of a deceased friend [Case No. 2]. S. H. Kelley also heard music, had an OOBE, and met an apparition [Case No. 3]. Kathleen Snowden heard music as she approached a new "world" during her OOBE [Case No. 4]. J. W. Skilton had an OOBE during which he *saw* music being sung by discarnates in "another world" [Case No. 13]. We have already pointed out that the music often accompanies deathbed visions, and music has been heard accompanying apparitions (possible inhabitants of the "next world"). On this basis alone we should expect that, *a priori,* the disclosures "communicators" make about music of the "next world" would be a logical excursion to embark upon for study.

It might also be pointed out that most psychical phenomena somehow fit into a survivalistic network: mediumship, apparitions, deathbed visions, and so on. Even such an innocuous feat as telepathy not only indicates survival of the human personality (according to such psychists as G. N. M. Tyrrell and Whately Carington) but is claimed to be *the* method of communication in the "next world."[1] Thus it is *logical* that psychic

---

[1] Professor H. H. Price has written several articles on a theoretical model for a post-mortem world. Some of his theories are backed up by mediumistic statements. While most of Professor Price's work has been published in parapsychological journals, a good resumé can be found in his chapter, "What Kind of Next World?" in the volume *Man's Concern with Death* (edited by Arnold Toynbee, St. Louis: McGraw-Hill, 1969).

music would also have a relationship. David Techter has pointed out concerning the music in his review of *NAD*, "Although it is consistent with the survival hypothesis, it is not compelling evidence" [*Fate*, April, 1971]. We will return to this remark later.

One of the first areas to cover would be what "communicators" say of music heard at their own deaths. Since deathbed music is one of the more frequent forms of NAD, certainly "communicators" should also report it. In our first volume we did cite one instance of this sort [Case No. 97], wherein a "communicator" reported, through the American medium, Mrs. Chamberlaine, that she heard singing during her death. We can now add more such cases.

Case No. 123 – "Alice"

This account of death was published in the *Journal* ASPR, August, 1907, as "A Remarkable Mediumistic Experience," and it included a preface by J. H. Hyslop. In the narrative, written automatically, "Alice," the "communicator," stated, "When I awoke [after going through death] the first thing that I became conscious of was the most magnificent singing that mortal ears ever listened to."

Certainly such a description is in keeping with the experiences of Mr. Skilton [Case No. 13].

Case No. 124 – "George Eliot"

This famous literary figure was alleged to communicate through the equally famous medium, Mrs. Piper (Henry Holt, *On the Cosmic Relations*. Boston: Houghton Mifflin Co., 1914). On March 6, 1897, "Eliot" communicated:

> The passing out of the spirit is like dropping off into a profound slumber for awhile . . . when my eyes were blinded and my ears ceased to hear, I felt a shadow of darkness passing over my whole frame. I was no longer conscious . . . this lasted from a few moments and I

121

awoke in a realm of golden light. I heard the voices of friends who had gone before calling to me to follow them. At that moment the thrill of joy was so intense I was like one standing spellbound before a beautiful panorama. *The music which filled my soul was like a tremendous symphony.* I had never heard or dreamed of anything half so beautiful . . . *the voices of my friends sounded like the soft mellow strains of a silver lute.* [Compare to Case No. 32, where the voices were likened to an Aeolian harp.]

Case No. 125 — Hodgson's "Cousin"

This case also comes from the Piper records cited in Case No. 124, and claimed to be from a cousin (deceased) of Richard Hodgson, one of Mrs. Piper's chief investigators. In reminiscing about her death, the cousin writes:

Oh what a beautiful place this is [the next world], so light, so really light . . . I have no pain. *Oh, I heard them singing and all to comfort me.*

Case No. 126 — "Mary Lodge"

This communication allegedly came from "Mary Lodge," wife of the famous psychical researcher, Oliver Lodge, and was received by the "Hamilton Circle" in Canada. The Hamilton Circle was a private group investigating physical and mental mediumship under the guidance of T. Glen Hamilton, and their findings were published in 1942 as *Intention and Survival* (Toronto: Macmillan Co.).

The following case is recorded in a new discussion of Hamilton's work, *Is Survival a Fact?* (London: Psychic Press, 1969) by Margaret Hamilton, Glen Hamilton's daughter. The Lodge script of 1933 reads:

The first clear recollection I had after my mortal eyes watched the anxious looks of my dear husband and children *was being borne upward by heavenly sweet music of welcome.*

The script goes on to tell of being met by deceased relatives, just as so many other accounts do.

Agreed, such cases, as Techter points out, are consistent with, but not evidence for, survival. Yet, what of these consistencies? In Case Nos. 124–25 "communicators" state that the music was related to those who came to comfort them in death. Certainly this is much in keeping with the remarks of Peter Nielsen [Case No. 37], who heard welcoming "angels" singing; Mrs. ――――, who heard singing accompanying her visions of welcoming figures [Case No. 38]; Fred ――――, who had similar experiences [Case No. 94], and "Sissy" [Case No. 96], who heard music and saw her deceased daughter coming to her as she died.

The two preceding communications which came through Mrs. Piper have special relevance in the light of such cases as Peter Nielsen, who reported that the music was produced *by* discarnates welcoming him to the "next world." These cases are not only *consistent* with the survival hypothesis but are also independently *corroborative* to ante-mortem deathbed visions. There are no inconsistencies in our collected data between music heard at deathbeds and music claimed to have been heard by "communicators" reported through mediums.

Our next area of consideration should be what "communicators" say about music in the afterlife. Just about every book on the afterlife has some descriptive matter concerning the music of that world. Consistent with what is reported by percipients of psychic music, "communicators" usually describe the music as either choral or orchestral, and usually as inconceivably more beautiful than anything ever heard on earth. For example, we find the following extract in *Light in Our Darkness* (London: Psychic Book Club, 1941):

> Presently, when their eyes are no longer dazzled by the exquisite scene, sounds of music seem to echo from

123

the sky and to float in the coloured atmosphere. You have music on earth, but perfect harmony is impossible in your present vibration. Your ears are not fine enough to realize this, but here the vibrations are made so delicate that a fractional difference of tone would strike one as discord. Imagine therefore an orchestra in which every instrument was perfect in tone and time. Even you would not realize what music might be.

From *The Way of Life* (London: Psychic Press) by Arthur Findlay:

Music was then discussed. A lady present asked if there was music in the world from which his friend was speaking: "Every sort of music you wish you can hear. There are many choirs who sing here, just the same as you sang on the Earth Plane."

From *Philip in the Spheres* (London: Psychic Book Club, n.d.):

. . . some activities are an extension of earth ones . . . music, painting. . . . can all be continued from where they are left off.

From *The Twentieth Plane* (London: Sampsenhamm Marston & Co., n.d.) by Albert Watson:

All the beautiful things that inspire and thrill our lives here, are there too. Art and Music, Poetry and the Drama . . . have there a home.

In our previous book we discussed a few other extracts, these being communications received through Mrs. Leonard.

As to the creation of music, it appears that music is generally either created on instruments or by thought. The latter theme crops up continually in these studies:

124

From *Across the Line* (New York: E. P. Dutton & Co., 1945) by Anice Terhune:

In response to how music is heard: "I let it flood my soul. I think the wish and then am there . . . but the music about me is more wonderfully beautiful than any music one hears on earth."

From *Philip in the Spheres* (London: Psychic Book Club, n.d.):

It is not easy to explain how thought creation works. Things which are of the essence of mind such as music and musical instruments function here admirably.

Oddly, there appear to be two different types of music in the "next world" according to "communicators"—the natural music created in the afterlife and, more interestingly, a type of mystical music which is apparently as supernormal to them as is NAD to us!

From *Philip in the Spheres:*

There is music. Not only when one seeks deliberately the music thought-world, but wondering strains and bars —thought creations of happy musically minded beings. Music seemed to be energy from each breath of air.

From *The Twentieth Plane:*

We hear far off the celestial choir singing the evening anthem.

Compare the following description of this "paranormal" music to our descriptions of NAD.

From *A Wanderer in Spirit Lands* (Chicago: Progressive Thinker Publishing House, 1901) by Franchezzo (translated by Fernie):

125

. . . A soft strain of music floated towards us as though borne upon some passing breeze. This grew stronger, fuller, more distinct, till a solemn majestic measure like the march of any army fell upon our ears.

. . . I beheld a glorious dazzling light as of a sun in splendor, shining as no mortal eye ever saw the sun shine on earth. And its rays dispelled the clouds of darkness and sorrow and I heard a glorious strain of music from the celestial spheres.

Note the crescendo effect of the music and the light. (These data are not inconsistent with music heard as part of an OOBE. "Communicators" talk of a "second death" from their world to a high world similar to our conception of mortal death.)

In all the preceding passages we find no inconsistencies. It is very difficult to evaluate this type of book, since no corroborative evidence is usually supplied; however, many do seem to show inner congruities with one another. Other references which provide such details are found in *From Four Who Are Dead* (by Dawson-Scott, 1926), *Life Worth Living* (Heslop), *Letters from Lancelot* (Anonymous, 1931), *Not Silent If Dead* (Fernie, 1890), *Opening the Psychic Door* (Fitzsimmons, 1933), *The Blue Island* (via Hester Dowden, 1922), *Love Conquers Death* (Vivian), *Raymond* (Oliver Lodge, 1916—the most famous of them all), *Claude's Book* (Bamber, 1918), *Letters from a Living Dead Man* (Barker, 1914), *Death's Door Ajar* (J.V.H., 1934), *After Death* (Stead, 1897), *Letters from the Other Side* (Anonymous, 1917), *Neither Dead nor Sleeping* (Sewall, 1921), *Private Dowding* (Pole, 1917).

As can be seen by the dates, most of these books were written during the great influx of belief in spiritualism prompted by the tragedy of World War I, especially after Sir Oliver Lodge's highly controversial *Raymond* (evidence and descriptions received through Mrs. Leonard). However the consistencies among them are so complex that it is inconceivable that they were "cribbed" from each other.

Before discussing the nature and significance of these descriptions of music in the "next world," I would like to outline one more recurring pattern.

In *NAD* I wrote (page 128):

> Obviously we have before us a phenomenon as old as man and one which is connected with religion—for have not music, painting and sculpture always been related to religious aesthetics, and has not religion always made use of art and music as an integral part of worship? I doubt if any musician has not, at least once, wondered: "Where does music come from?" The question is not as superficial as might be thought, for many philosophers as well as musicians have echoed this very inquiry.

When I wrote those lines I was toying with the idea that earthly music might have had its origins in the ancients, who may have heard psychic music. Or, in fact, that NAD is the prototype upon which music is based. Oddly I found this same theme reappearing in spiritualist literature.

From *Across the Line:*

> All the really good music originates here and is sent down to earth to use in your earth medium.

From *Philip in the Spheres:*

> You must realise that it has its communities; people of a fairly advanced type who have common interests and have learnt the art of thought creation; have united their thought force to form better "worlds" like that garden in the Hall of Music . . . then they can inspire, by telepathy, people on earth to take up the same idea.

From *The Twentieth Plane:*

> . . . The Universe, as a lullaby to its soul, has a song that it forever sings, and when your inspiration vibrates

in regular time with this greater song, you, too, hear music which you express.

From *A Wanderer in the Spirit Lands:*

. . . They [mortals] heard the wondrous music and tried to give it expression . . . and these mortals were termed geniuses . . . for all that is highest and purest and best comes from the inspiration of the spirit world.[2]

One must say that, if we accept survival, this theory is as workable as any other. Many philosophers and musicologists have pondered the question of the origins of music:—Why and how did music develop in the early history of man? Interestingly, music had its greatest development as a form of art within the church. Actually, though, nobody has ever come up with an acceptable theory on the subject. Rousseau and Spencer thought that music originated from "heightened speech," and Walaschik felt music to have arisen from rhythmic pulses. Other theories have been put forth by Carl Stumpf and Curt Sachs and others. These various theories range from music having arisen as a means of emotional expression to man's desire to imitate bird songs. Pythagoras, of course, considered music to have a supernatural basis in the frequencies emitted by the movements of the heavenly bodies. Considering all the evidence of NAD, could not music have had a supernormal source? We note that the music heard during supernormal states was perceived predominantly as either choral or like an organ. During the early development of liturgical music only choral and organ music was considered fit for religious use, and all other musical media were banned from performance within the Church. Indeed an interesting parallel: Were the sounds of singing and the organ devised to imitate psychic music?

----

[2] This quotation reminds one of the feverish way Handel wrote his *Messiah.* Also, Tschaikovsky as a young child heard mystical music, subjectively, and was much terrified by the experience.

Again, the most prominent feature of these cases is that there are no inconsistencies in the descriptions of psychic music heard by selected individuals in normal states, during OOBEs, or near death. Further, these descriptions tally with accounts of deathbed music reported by the "dead" and about music in the "next world."

We can now return to the major criticisms which were elaborated in the review in *Fate* by David Techter:

> Some years ago the noted comedian Jack Benny starred in a mediocre movie titled, "The Horn Blows at Midnight." In the film there was a long dream sequence in which Jack Benny imagined himself to be a trumpet player in a heavenly orchestra—rank after rank of white-robed musicians eternally performing music of adoration. This portrait of Heaven was based on a stereotyped tradition reaching back to the dawn of the New Testament and likely millennia earlier. And it seems to me this tradition is the major problem in the interpretation of NAD experiences. Rogo argues (in the fashion of Robert Crookall, whose writings he admires) that the concordance between independent accounts can only be explained by the assumption that the reported experiences have an objective basis rather than that they are hallucinatory. He presents evidence that there indeed are similarities between the reports but the alternate explanation, obviously, is that these similarities are due to their derivation from the same tradition of heavenly music . . . the hearing of heavenly choruses or orchestras well may be due to expectancy on the part of those who experience this . . . .
>
> Thus, I tend to disagree with Rogo's inclination to regard NAD as evidence for survival. To be sure, it is consistent with the survival hypothesis but scarcely compelling evidence.
>
> Crookall's line of argument is far more persuasive in the case of astral projection, for here there is no widespread tradition relating or affecting the phenomena.

129

Indeed most persons never have heard of anyone leaving his body, whereas nearly everyone has heard of angel choruses. Perhaps it would be more pertinent to ask why NAD cases are so rare!

I find it no problem to respond to the above criticism. Offhand I think a perfect "chicken-egg" type problem has been outlined. While there is an inclination to believe that psychic music may have originated from a cultural tradition, it is just as feasible to accept that this undefined "cultural tradition" came, in fact, from ancient observations of the phenomena! Thus, the basic premise is an arbitrary one with little evidential support.

The second point is that these patterns may have roots in a cultural tradition. This criticism has more of a basis than the first, since, regardless of origin, we do have a tradition of "heavenly music," which can be seen in Flemish art with all the brilliant paintings of heavenly choirs and harp-strumming angels.[3] However, I cannot see how this tradition can account for the *patterns* we have found. Indeed if all our cases described choral music just at death, the point would be a damaging one;

___

[3] From Robert Crookall's *Events on the Threshold of the After-Life* (1967): "Connected with the conception of ascending into heaven was the practice of Medieval artists of depicting 'saints' sitting in clouds and playing harps (see Rev. XIV, 2). Nothing has caused greater derision. Nevertheless such productions are understandable. Many people who suffered pseudo-death and many astral projectors state—quite independently of mediums—that they heard sweet sounds and these they not unnaturally called 'music.' Many of those who have left the body permanently, i.e. the 'dead,' made the same statement (through mediums). Medieval artists who presumably never had, or at least never 'remembered' having had any out-of-the-body experiences when quite well (i.e. astral projections) or exceedingly ill (i.e. pseudo-death) naturally supposed that 'music' is producible only by means of instruments. Combining this (unwarranted) deduction with the actual observation that the released Soul Body ascends, they depicted 'angels' *as sitting* on clouds and playing harps. Those who derive amusement from this confusion should remember that admixtures of unwarranted deductions with correct observations are by no means unknown in modern medicine and the biological and psychological sciences [page 151].

130

however, "cultural traditions" do not explain the crescendo effect of the music, why music heard in natural OOBEs is different from music heard in enforced OOBEs, and why music is sometimes heard as choral and sometimes as instrumental. None of the new patterns discussed in this volume can be explained away by the argument of "cultural tradition." The fact that collective experiences have been recorded has been overlooked —and this immediately places the phenomena on an entirely different level. Cultural traditions do not explain collective cases!

This negates the criticism that music may be heard due to some expectancy on the part of the percipient. If expectancy is a possible source for *hallucinatory* music (and certainly *not* collectively perceived cases), then we should expect that music heard by the dying should be reported in studies of deathbed experiences. However, when Osis presented his huge study, *Deathbed Observations by Physicians and Nurses* (Parapsychology Foundation, 1961), there was no mention of deathbed music. Either Osis found nothing in his study, or his findings in this specific area were too negligible and so were dismissed. Certainly if there is a cultural tradition affecting these cases, the phenomenon would have come to Osis's attention. Conversely, these cases actually seem to be so rare that they cannot be fitted into a cultural artifact model.

I also must disagree that the cultural tradition of angelic music is greater than that for the OOBE. There is a huge amount of evidence that the OOBE has been known in all cultures. The neo-Platonists had a tradition of the OOBE (see Mead's *The Subtle Body in Western Tradition*), as do the Tibetans (see my study of this in Volume X of the *International Journal of Parapsychology*). Actually, wherever a culture exists in which survival of death is a widespread belief, invariably a tradition of the soul and a soul-body is also present. This, however, in no way argues against the reality of the OOBE. As I have said before, we cannot really argue whether psychical phenomena come from cultural traditions or if these traditions come from the existence of psychical phenomena!

On the other hand, there is very little tradition regarding

131

heavenly music. I will agree that the Bible talks of heavenly music (in a totally different concept than NAD), the Tibetans have a belief in a musical sphere in the other-world, and the ancient Greeks believed in the Music of the Spheres. However, the argument that the NAD experiences we have recorded come from such vague beliefs and traditions is futile, since it cannot explain the patterns that the music follows or the interrelationship it has to other psychical phenomena.

Finally, I would like to comment on the statement that psychic music is "consistent with the survival hypothesis but scarcely compelling evidence" by elaborating what I touched upon at the beginning of the chapter.

What, if any, case for survival can we make from these case studies? We do not have any clear-cut case to demonstrate survival after death, but we do find remarkable patterns which seem to point in the direction of survival after death.

The cases contained herein and in the previous book on this topic show that some persons often hear music as they lie dying, and on a few occasions this music has been heard collectively. In this study we have demonstrated that the "dead," through mediums, have described music *they* heard while dying. This alone is a significant parallel. It is of even greater importance that the description of the music does not vary between accounts by the living or the "dead."

While this seems to indicate that the "communications" may have a post-mortem source, it does not give direct evidence that the music heard is a property of the "next world." However, there is clear inferential support. Now, taking the descriptions of (1) psychic music heard by the living and (2) music reported to be heard *before and after* death by the "dead," and comparing these to (3) the music which discarnates claim *is* a property of their world, *we find no significant inconsistencies.*

It is hard to believe that all these concordances exist by chance. As has been argued in the previous pages, these descriptions could not be explained as being based on a cultural tradition, since while such a source *might* explain why hallucinatory music could be sensed by the dying (and even this is speculation), it does not explain (1) why this music is heard similarly at death and during the OOBE, (2) pattern recurrences which *can* be explained on a psychic theory, (3) why it is heard collectively, and (4) why these same patterns are reported by the "dead."

It must also be borne in mind that the "communications" we have drawn upon represent not only popular spiritualist books but utterances and transcripts from Mrs. Piper and Mrs. Leonard. The importance of their mediumships as evidence for survival of bodily death cannot be overstated and need not be outlined in this volume.[4] Some of the statements concerning music in the "next world" outlined in both this book and touched upon in the first volume of *NAD* were taken from sittings which, apart from the descriptive material, gave strong evidence of survival of personality. To accept the "communications" but overlook the descriptive data given is illogical. Agreed that the process of transmitting data through a "medium" causes coloring by the medium's mind, all these descriptions of the

---

[4] For the Piper material, refer to *Proc.* SPR, Vol. VIII, Pt. XXI; Vol. XIII, Pt. 5; Vol. XIV, Pt. XXXIV; Vol. XVI, Pt. XLI; Vol. XVII, Pt. XLV; Vol. XXII, Pt. LVII; Vol. XXIII, Pt. LVIII; Vol. XXIV, Pt. LXI; Vol. XXVIII, Pt. LXX. These represent the main volumes in the SPR proceedings. As for books on Mrs. Piper, refer to M. Sage, *Mrs. Piper and the S.P.R.* (1903); Alta Piper's *The Life and Work of Mrs. Piper* (1929); and Anne Robbins' *Both Sides of the Veil* (1909) and *Past and Present with Mrs. Piper* (1922).

For the Leonard material, refer to *Proc.* SPR: Allison (Vol. XLI); Besterman (Vol. XL); Carrington (Vol. XLII, Vol. XLIII, Vol. XLV); Newton (Vol. XLV); Radclyffe-Hall and Una, Lady Troubridge (Vol. XXX); Salter (Vol. XXXIII, Vol. XXXVI, Vol. XXXIX); Sidgewick (Vol. XXXI); Thomas (Vol. XXXVIII, XLII, XLV, XLVIII); Troubridge (Vol. XXXII, XXXIV). See also Allison's *Leonard and Soule Experiments in Psychical Research* (1929); Glenconner's *The Earthen Vessel* (1921); Lodge's *Raymond* (1916); Thomas's *Some New Evidence for Human Survival* (1922) and *Life Beyond Death with Evidence* (1928); Nea Walker's *The Bridge* (1927) and *Through a Stranger's Hands* (1935); and for an easy-to-read survey, Susy Smith's *The Mediumship of Mrs. Leonard* (1966).

music of the "next world" are so greatly in agreement that they cannot be easily dismissed.

In the light of these sets of data, it appears that psychic music is a property of the "next world" and that those who perceive it during their mortal state do so during times such as death or the OOBE, when they are brought closer to the "next world."

Chapter 7

The Final Question

There is now only one other question to be considered: What are the mechanics of the phenomenon? To understand this I should explain why the music is almost always heard in conjunction with the OOBE, why persons hear the music differently from each other, and why the music can also be heard apparently independently of the OOBE.

In *NAD* I suggested the use of an ether model similar to various theories expounded by H. H. Price,[1] Raynor Johnson,[2] and W. G. Roll.[3] All three have postulated the existence of a psychic ether (even though the ether model as used in physics has been pronounced obsolete, the use of the model applied to psychical phenomena is not quite the same thing) which acts as a mediator between the subjective world of thoughts and ideas and the objective world of matter—between sense perception and psychic perception. In my interpretation the psychic

---

[1] Price, H. H.: Presidential Address to the S.P.R., 1939.

[2] Johnson, Raynor: *The Imprisoned Splendour* (New York: Harper, 1953).

[3] Roll, W. G.: "The Psi Field Theory" (Presidential Address: The Seventh Annual Conference of the Parapsychological Association).

ether becomes the border between this world and the "next world."

By far the most active promoter of the ether theory is Dr. Raynor Johnson, an Australian physicist. Johnson views the ether as both physical and nonphysical:

> This [the ether] must partake of some of the qualities of matter such as the occupation of space and a degree of permanence of form, and it must also have qualities akin to mind in sustaining and carrying emotions and thought-images. This psychic aether is malleable and moulded by matter so that it forms what might be called aetheric duplicates. A truer statement would perhaps be that the aetheric duplicate is the model on which the material structure is condensed. It is this aetheric duplicate which the mind apprehends in clairvoyance and through which it manipulates matter in psychokinesis and materialization phenomena. On the other hand, the psychic aether linked with a material object can be impregnated with mental characteristics i.e. with emotionally toned ideas. . . . This hypothesis of a psychic aether is a unifying one of considerable range and power; it bridges the gap between matter and mind, and becomes a convenient vehicle for interpreting all these para-normal phenomena.[4]

If we accept survival of death, then it is not hard to accept that, just as all physical objects have an etheric prototype, so would man himself—demonstrable in the OOBE where the "etheric" body is projected—and from this we can postulate that our world has an etheric base. While this may sound like over-theorizing, modern physics holds the concept of the "parallel universe" to be a logical hypothesis. And there is little difference between a "parallel" universe and an etheric one.[5]

---

[4] *Op. cit.*, Johnson, pp. 28–29.

[5] See Johnson's *The Imprisoned Splendour* for a complete discussion of the psychic ether.

All psychical phenomena can be explained as working through the psychic ether. Telepathy is a reflection off the ether shield; clairvoyance is direct contact with the ether; precognition and retrocognition are the readings of traces in the movement of the ether; and physical phenomena move *along* the ether field, which is why they may break the laws of physics.

The ether is, as I said, that field which separates the world of the living from the world of the dead. That is why it maintains properties of both mind and matter—just as gelatine has properties of both liquid and solid. Just as glass is actually a slow-moving liquid which takes on the properties of matter when a rock is hurled through it, so the ether, though intangible, may take on physical properties when it is activated by a psychic sense.

The principle of etheric duplicates has had a long history in parapsychology, and the concept has some empirical foundation. It has long been noted that during poltergeist outbreaks great crashes are heard, yet no objects are displaced; dishes are heard being toppled, yet on investigation all is found in order. To explain these uncanny effects, psychical researchers postulated "astral matter," which is, in effect, this concept of etheric duplication.[6] Early theorists also had suppositions of "astral eyes" at work in clairvoyance and "astral ears" to explain clairaudience. Although the terminology has changed and theories are now draped in symbolic logic, mathematical formulae, and so on, they still are little different from those bygone conjectures.

The OOBE is a prime example of the etheric duplicate. Although many parapsychologists refuse to commit themselves as to whether or not the OOBE demonstrates the existence of an etheric body, Crookall's books and analyses certainly demonstrate the likelihood, since no theory of "body image" can explain the "double" perceived—so it seems to show that the

---

[6] Refer to Hornell Hart: *Toward a New Philosophical Basis for Parapsychological Phenomena* (New York: Parapsychology Foundation).

"double" does have a physical or superphysical reality.[7] Unfortunately the data which Hornell Hart and Robert Crookall amassed were sorely neglected by parapsychologists.[8]

By this general theory we can see the significance of mediumistic communications which suggest that our music is an echo of their "other-world" music. Since all things have an etheric prototype, it is feasible that music, too, would have a superphysical base—and certainly this etheric music would be more common to an etheric world than to our own coarse universe. (These ideas can be found in Hindu and Buddhist writings also.) Thus, the statements by "communicators" are altogether consistent with our ether-model.

Every day we are bombarded constantly by sounds. In fact, persons placed under sensory deprivation, where they can hear *no* sounds, soon find the state intolerable. Psychic music is not heard by the physical sense of hearing—this we demonstrated in a previous chapter. It is heard by an etheric organ, and this etheric organ is a property of the etheric body. This is the first reason that psychic music is linked to the OOBE, for during the OOBE our perceptions are a mixture of the "real" world and of the etheric world. This is why during the experience some individuals see "earth scenes" while others are transported to "etheric scenes." Psychic music is a property of the etheric world and thus, during the OOBE, just as one might "see" scenes of this world and the next, so he might "hear" sounds of this world as well as the next. In reading many accounts of the experience, one is struck by the fact that many describe physical objects as "glowing." This is evidence that they may be seeing

---

[7] See Crookall: *Mechanisms of Astral Projection* (Moradabad, 1969); *The Jung-Jaffé View of Out-of-the-Body Experiences* (London: World Fellowship Press, 1970); and *Out-of-the-Body Experiences: A Fourth Analysis* (New Hyde Park, N.Y.: University Books, 1970).

[8] Hart, Hornell: "A Chasm Needs to Be Bridged" (Journal: ASPR, 1968); "Scientific Survival Research" (*International Journal of Parapsychology*, Vol. IX).

by a new mechanism and therefore seeing the etheric properties upon which physical matter is based. Therefore, hearing psychic music is the perceiving of a sensory experience from the "next world."

Now, we must ask, why at deathbeds are collective cases heard and why do the various witnesses hear the music at different levels? But first it should be noted that it is not unique only to psychic music that the various witnesses seem to experience the same manifestation at different levels of perception. This phenomenon is noted with visual manifestations as well. For instance, Sir William Crookes, in his famous *Researches in the Phenomena of Spiritualism*, writes of the physical mediumship of D. D. Home:

> . . . . a flower or other small object is seen to move; one person present will see a luminous cloud hovering over it, another will detect a nebulous looking hand, whilst others will see nothing at all but the moving flower.

This observation by Crookes is uniquely parallel to what we noted about psychic music.

Obviously, we cannot perceive the properties of the "next world" directly by our physical organism. During an OOBE the etheric double can perceive these properties and relay them to the physical senses. When a death takes place, a very complex type of OOBE also takes place—a permanent release from the physical body, a projection from our world to the next. During a death experience all individuals around the dying person come into contact with the psychic ether, which is being activated by the projection taking place. Thus all who are at the deathbed come into contact with the ether and may hear psychic music reflected off the psychic ether. We all have different levels of perception—some of us have better hearing than others, some better eyesight and so on. There is no reason to suppose that we all have the same psychic sense perception. We know

139

that some persons are gifted subjects, while others may go through life without ever having a psychic experience. Therefore, when a large body of persons witness a death, they all might hear psychic music at distinct levels of perception based on their individual attunement to the psychic ether. A more "psychic" individual would hear the music at a high level, such as hearing voices singing distinct words, while a poor subject might either hear faint music or nothing at all. In the case of the famous Morton Ghost of Cheltenham,[9] the phantom appeared to have physical characteristics but was visible to some members of the household but not to others. This too is analogous to what we have discovered about psychic music. It answers our final question as to why music is sometimes heard without any intimation that an OOBE might be taking place, such as during the Welsh Revival. For during periods of great emotional, religious, and spiritual activity, a certain "collective psychism" (to borrow René Sudre's term) might be kindled. This would cause some activation of the psychic ether, which may manifest itself haphazardly, thus displaying the properties of the "next world" momentarily to our world.

The ether model has an old heritage in parapsychology and, although there can never be "proof" of its existence, many observations point to its reality. *If* man survives death—and a great amount of psychic phenomena points in that direction—there must be a borderline between our world and the next. And, just as two inclined planes join to create an infinite line, so must there be a point where the world of mind joins the world of matter. Psychical phenomena point to such an ether—apparitions often display both physical and nonphysical characteristics—and our world-view of a separate world of subjective ideas and physical qualities is inadequate to account for such phenomena.[10]

---

[9] Morton, Rose: "Record of a Haunted House" (*Proc:* S.P.R., Vol. VIII).

[10] Dividing our world into subjective and objective qualities is actually a Western tradition. One of the main points of Buddhist

But more important than philosophy or theory is the empirical application of the ether model. The model has been used by H. H. Price to explain hauntings, and by Raynor Johnson as an explanatory model for telepathy, clairvoyance, and physical phenomena. Psychic music is also most applicable to the ether theory, and the theory adequately explains all the diversified patterns and exceptions we have noted in this case study.

The world of psychic phenomena is a baffling one—a world of contradictions and a world beyond man's myopic view of his own universe. The universe is limitless and man, in trying to place arbitrary restrictions on its laws and manifestations, only betrays his ignorance. In this world of psychic phenomena, to find any theoretical model to explain the assorted bits and pieces of data, laboratory experiments, and field observations, is close to the alchemist's quest for the philosopher's stone. The ether model *does* place psychic phenomena in an organized, meaningful scheme. Can any theory offer more?

---

philosophy is that there is no difference between subjective and objective, and both are merely products of man's categorical reasoning, which is a product of his own ignorance.

Conclusions:

NAD, Death, and the Ecstasy of Experience

All our discussions have a crucial bearing on one important point: to view death as a total experience instead of in negative terms of termination. If man survives death, and I feel the great complexity and interrelation of all psychical phenomena compel us to admit to this conviction, then the death experience itself must be looked upon as a transcendental experience —a complete experience in that we survive, and the experience then affects the progressing personality. I do not plan to argue the entire issue of survival of death. This has adequately been done in other volumes which invariably come to an optimistic conclusion: Hornell Hart's *Enigma of Survival*, W. H. Salter's *Zoar*, and Paul Beard's *Survival of Death*. Of course, we cannot speak in terms of "proof," since proof is largely a subjective creation in the mind of the evaluator and a critic of survival will never be satisfied that his criteria for "proof" have been met, even though his arguments have a marked tendency *not* to fulfill the same conditions he has set for his opposition.[1]

---

[1] For example, George Zorab in a paper, "The Survival Hypothesis: An Unsupported Speculation?" (*Journal: A.S.P.R.*, Vol. 60, No. 3), argues that all attempts at proving survival have failed and that in any

Personally I believe one cannot isolate one psychic phenomenon from another. We cannot ask, "How does mediumistic communication serve as evidence for survival?" and "How do apparitions fit into the mosaic?" and then "What is the importance of deathbed visions to the question?" It is no wonder that, in the light of these types of categorical arguments, many feel the enigma of survival is still an open question. We must view all paranormal phenomena in terms of the others in order to find any unitary significance to the genres.

For example, Hornell Hart in his "Six Theories about Apparitions" (*Proceedings* SPR, Vol. L) showed that apparitions of the living (ostensible OOBEs) are of the same nature as apparitions of the dead. Therefore, one cannot discuss one without discussing the other. Likewise, mediums entering trance undergo experiences similar to the OOBE. Again, we find a relationship. Similarly clairvoyants at deathbeds see the "soul leaving the body" in the same manner as people who have had the OOBE describe the experience. To take this a step further, the "dead" discuss their experience of dying in the same terms as those who have had the OOBE. All these interrelationships must be considered when evaluating survival. The greatest advent in the development of psychology was the shift toward *gestalt* theory wherein it was felt a more comprehensive picture of the human organism could be found by viewing the entire being in terms of "wholeness" instead of as a study of individual systems. Such a need exists in parapsychology, especially in the study of death. One can argue successfully against any one form of psychical phenomenon as evidence for survival. However, this does not mean that these arguments can explain why there are connections between various psychic phenomena. Let us take the NAD experience. Certainly we could argue that persons having subjective NAD experiences were hallucinated

event survival is so against biological data that the concept can be dismissed. As Roll replies ("Concluding Remarks" in the A.S.P.R. Survival Symposium under which Zorab's paper appeared), the same argument could hold true for *all* Psi phenomena, including those which Zorab feels are adequate to explain survival evidence.

on the evidence of that one body of cases. We could go on to explain the similarities in the reports as consequences of a similar form of delusion. However, by doing so, we would be ignoring the fact that collectively heard cases are also described in the same terms as those occurring personally and that the same characteristics governing one body of cases which *could be dismissed* also apply to that body of cases which *cannot be dismissed*. One group gives corroborative evidence to the other.

Where do all these cases lead us? Where are the most perfect cases heard? Our criteria for the "perfect" music case would have to fit these general criteria: (1) It was heard by all in the general area where the phenomenon occurred, (2) it would be heard *generally* in the same manner by everyone (I say generally because we all perceive in different ways and especially in terms of psychic perception), and such cases fulfilling these requirements always occur related to death.

This point illustrates my argument that only in relation to death and survival of death does the large body of psychic phenomena have any meaning. What is telepathy if not the means man will use to communicate after his death which on occasion manifests in life? What is clairvoyance if not a faculty we will use after death? What is precognition if not that faculty which is beyond the time factor man has set *arbitrarily* for himself in this world but may not be a "law" in the next world? What is the OOBE if not that mode of permanent release for the physical body at the time of death?

If we grade all psychical phenomena in order of complexity they invariably lead us to the death phenomena. Telepathy is the communication of thought which overcomes the factor of space. Precognition is that psychic faculty that corrupts our concept of time. Now these factors all lead to mediumship, which is telepathy between the living and dead where both the concepts of time and space are nullified. One phenomenon can only be seen in terms of the others. Similarly, NAD experiences also follow these same gradings, becoming more complex and perfect as we come closer to the death experience.

I can see little meaning in the entire realm of psychical phenomena unless they are viewed in the light of survival of death and man's ability to affect life on this world after death. What antisurvivalists lack is not logic, but insight. Knowing *about* psychic phenomena does not bring insight, and such issues as the difficulty of conceiving a life after death or *a priori* arguments from psychology or physics are very phony issues.

Most likely my view comes from the fact that psychical research has always been my main concern, and my academic training has been in a totally unrelated field. My background in psychology, religion, philosophy, and the sciences was dependent on my interest in psychical research and not the other way around. Most parapsychologists have an initial training in psychology, philosophy, and related fields, and only after their academic training became interested in this field. This being so, they have inevitably found themselves viewing psychical phenomena in the light of what they have been trained in—and because of this can only see psychic phenomena in respect to the problems of such disciplines as psychology, physics, and philosophy, and, of course, the concept of survival is paradoxical to many of the "accepted" teachings of these disciplines. The problem, however, is not with psychical phenomena, but with these disciplines themselves. We cannot limit the implications of psychical phenomena because of the imperfect knowledge that we have of science and psychology. These studies will have to be reanalyzed in the light of parapsychology. It is here that many parapsychologists—especially antisurvivalists—make their mistake. They fail to see psychical research as a self-contained study but bias it by their preconceived ideas, and then try to mold the implications of parapsychology into the framework of their other academic disciplines. These disciplines add relatively little to our knowledge of psychical phenomena, but psychical phenomena add greatly to our infant knowledge of science, philosophy, and psychology.

I do not mean these remarks to be considered a full exposition of my feelings toward survival of death. Such an examination would take hundreds of pages to complete. The point I am attempting to make, and I can already see certain of my colleagues sorrowfully shaking their heads, is that we must look at psychical phenomena in terms of meaning and purpose and with a full appreciation of their ideological implications. And I can only see one teleological importance to them—survival of death.

A related factor is that the very existence of psychical phenomena deeply affects our view of death. People who undergo the out-of-the-body experience near death invariably report a new outlook toward life and death. We read such statements as, "The knowledge I gained at that time assured me of a future life"; "It makes me feel certain that there is a life after death, which does not require a material body for us to be able to see and hear, and that we shall retain our personality"; "Death is like passing from twilight into the glories of the full midday sunshine"; "I know that death does not end all"; "I was always afraid to die, but not now"; "To me there is nothing truer than 'there is no death' "; "There is no doubt in my mind [that] there is a life after death and a soul to our body"; "This experience convinced me of a future after death and gave me everlasting faith."[2]

Certainly a new meaning of death occurred to these people because they had the OOBE. Other percipients have made such remarks as that they were never the same after the experience.

Comments like this bring us back to a discussion earlier in this volume on the relationship of mystical experience and psychical experience, wherein I argued that the main difference is not so much in *characteristic* as in *degree*. I also argued that the psychical experience was a cognitive one. However, we must admit that here, too, it is a matter of degree for, while psychical experiences give us cognition of earthly things or "properties" such as apparitions and music of "the next world," mystical experiences give us a different degree of cognition— not of "properties" but of "knowledge" of cosmic and unitary mechanisms of the universe. People who undergo the OOBE and who claim to have new insight into the ways of life and death come close to meeting this criterion.

---

[2] Crookall: Case Nos. 2, 7, 17, 27, 309, 313, 342, 346.

147

It is because of this that I feel death is a merging of both the psychical and mystical experience. It is a transcendental event, and the knowledge we gain from it is of a nature we could never experience in our temporal bodies. Our physical organism limits us and chains us to our physical organs of perception, which we have come unconsciously to believe are our only means of gaining knowledge. Since death is an OOBE of a permanent nature, it is not odd that temporary OOBEs seem to serve the gap between the psychic and the mystical. One percipient wrote, "I suddenly found myself out of the body, floating over a moor in a body lighter than air. A cool wind was blowing. . . . I did not mind the wind as I should have done had I been in my physical body, because I was at one with it. The life in the wind and the clouds and the trees was within me also.[3]

"Starr Dailey" wrote in prison of the experience, "The joy, bliss and gratitude I felt was past articulation. . . . I knew I must either be changed or die. . . . I knew I had transcended all personal and bodily limitations. . . . I had no sense of my prison walls, but my thoughts roamed the imponderable Universe far and clear. The measurement of time and space vanished out of my consciousness. I knew that I was being 'reborn.' "[4]

Such experiences merge closely into the true mystical experience. "Starr Dailey's" experience, in fact, meets the requirements of unitary consciousness, nontemporality, and nonspatiality, which are the most distinguishing factors of the mystical experience. Since OOBEs often have psychical concomitants, here we have the bridge between the two.[5]

Such mystical enlightenments are also described by persons communicating after death. Private Dowding, in the classic

---

[3] In Raynor Johnson's *Watcher on the Hills* (London: Hodder & Stoughton, 1959).

[4] "Starr Dailey": *Release* (Arthur Jones, 1954).

[5] Again, reference for many of these general ideas can be found in Crookall's *The Interpretation of Cosmic and Mystical Experience* (London: James Clarke, 1969).

book of the same name by W. Tudor-Pole, communicated, "I am where I am, yet I am everywhere! I am a self that is far greater and vaster than what I thought and felt myself to be."

These types of transcendental experiences give us the answer to the meaning of death and how psychical processes affect that meaning. The mystical experience is not a rare gift or a rare occurrence. It is an experience we all are destined to have—and this mystical experience is death itself.

Appendix A

Dubious and Pseudo NAD Cases

In our survey of cases I explained that, because the material used in *NAD* contained certain patterns which seemed to govern the phenomena, we were able to sift out dubious cases so that the "index of cases" included in this volume could be of a higher level than those presented in the first volume. I also pointed out that many cases were not used in our present survey because of obvious fabrication or lack of detail.

However, one criticism was made that deserves a reply—in concordance with the patterns discovered in *NAD*, could it be that in compiling this current collection I avoided many cases which did not fit into these patterns, giving the patterns more evidential weight than they should have? This is an extremely touchy point and one I have brought out myself in a paper on the use of content analysis and pattern analysis:

> The major problem in this method [pattern analysis] of evaluation is the use of content analysis *selectively* in support of a bias. . . . The one major problem with using content analysis is the natural tendency to pick and choose only those cases which seem to fit a researcher's bias *and then pass off incomplete data as*

content analysis. . . . Because of this reason, a researcher must never attempt content analysis with a bias of *looking for a specific pattern* in his initial study of his data. Once certain patterns become obvious then other cases can be evaluated against an existing body of data.[1]

This is precisely what I have done in these two books on psychic music. I used virtually all the cases I received in the first volume, but for this second book I have disqualified some cases which I received. However, my criterion for this was not arrived at by use of pattern analysis but because many of them bordered on the absurd, and some were definitely caused by normal means.

But since this point is an important one, I here give capsule reviews of some of the many cases I have on file which were not included as examples of ostensibly genuine NAD experiences. Thus the reader can see how most of these cases are far from resembling the cases presented as evidence and why others were eliminated.

1. Case of Mrs. S.L.T. Mrs. T. claimed to hear the music for a period of years as though a tape were playing over and over. The musical content of the experience consisted of such songs as "Calling for You, for Me," "How I Love Jesus," "Go Tell Aunt Nabbie Her Old Gray Goose Is Dead," and several others. Notice in our cases that such a mundane level is hardly reached!

2. An unsigned report (one reason for disqualification) tells of hearing opera music in a graveyard. In trying to discover the source of the music, the subject noticed that, when he approached the music, it suddenly shifted to a different point. Thus, he relates, he chased the music all around the cemetery. Our own cases are rather encompassing, and none of the percipients describe the music as either operatic or as changing direction.

3. Case of Miss L.M. This could have been a genuine exam-

---

[1] Rogo, D. Scott: "Content Analysis as Evidence in Parapsychology" (*Parapsychology Review*, Vol. 2, No. 4).

ple, but was disqualified for several reasons. Miss L.M. describes how she heard organ music "for about two hours every afternoon and then at dusk" for two weeks before her mother's death. This type of lengthy duration is at odds with most of our data. However, unlike our cases, Miss M. did not find the experience at all divine. As she says, "I can tell you, Mr. Rogo, I sincerely detest organ music . . . it's psychic music I suppose —out of this world and, as far as I am concerned, that's exactly where it belongs!" Because of the duration of the music, it is feasible that it might have been caused by a radio or even an electrical appliance picking up music from a radio broadcast. Such cases have occurred.[2] In fact, there have been cases of people hearing music in their homes which emanated from another house projected by underground streams flowing under both houses and acting as a soundingboard from the original source.

4. Case of Mr. H. Mr. H. heard a voice which sang to him. The voice, according to Mr. H., claimed to identify itself as King Leviathan of the Deep!

5. Case of Mrs. Y. Again, this might have had a normal source or might have been a true experience. The experiencer, Mrs. Y., claimed to have heard a harmonica playing "Humoresque" after a neighbor died. Since she was so young at the time, and the music could have had a normal cause, especially since it was a rendering of a familiar musical composition, the case was rejected.

6. Case of Mr. C. This narrative could very well have been a genuine case of NAD heard during an OOBE. Mr. C. wrote: "When I was a small boy eight years old, I was very sick with the measles and scarlet fever both at the same time. I remember being so awfully sick that I could hear beautiful organ music playing and saw a man that I believe was 'God.' He stood on a rock holding out his hand to me. It seemed that I was in a

---

[2] I once turned on a tape machine though no tape was on it. If anyone touched the machine, loud music would be emitted, coming from a commercial broadcasting station.

valley surrounded with green grass and flowers. Had I reached out to take 'God's' hand, I know I would have died."

This experience might have been an OOBE, some of which include a "change of environment" to the beautiful "Paradise" condition. Also the figure seen is similar to beckoning and rejecting figures seen during OOBEs—especially those occurring near death. However, since Mr. C. had no direct remembrance of "leaving the body" and was so ill at the time, it could not be ruled out that the entire experience was due to delirium. It was therefore rejected.

7. Case of K.M.N. Mr. N. claimed to have heard what he called "celestial music" during an accidental encounter with a fallen power line. However, Mr. N. claimed that it was only after having touched the wire *for a period of time* that he gradually became shocked by the live wire. Also, he claimed that his hand was only "slightly" burned by the experience. Since this story stretches credulity a bit far, it was rejected. Had the narrator really touched a live wire with a piece of metal as he claims, he would have been instantly and severely shocked.

8. Case of Mr. K. Mr. K., a professional musician and arranger, sent in a letter describing some of his experience in trying to "hear" the music he wished to compose. Although interesting, the subject matter of the letter was not within the range of the present volume.

9. Case of Miss D.B. This report may very well have been genuine. It did describe the music in similar terms to the examples cited in our case studies. However, a colleague informed me that this same subject had been involved in a bogus case he investigated, so I thought it better to exclude Miss D.B.'s report. This subject also wished to be paid for the use of her experience, unlike *any* of the other correspondents.

10. Case of Mrs. J.B. Mrs. B. wrote saying, along with two pages of biography, that all night long she could hear hymns her mother used to sing.

11. Case of E. W. Mrs. W. sent a case describing how she hears sacred songs, audible all night, which are amplified when she

turns on the window fan. Apparently no one else hears the music, which she also experiences while driving her car. Again, if not a delusion, it seems likely that the music has a normal cause.

12. Case of Mrs. J.O. At first inspection this case was of some interest, since Mrs. O. described hearing "heavenly music" during an OOBE. However, in my follow-up I learned that Mrs. O. claims to have had OOBEs into outer space and to the bottom of the ocean, and "mystical" experience by the dozens. Mrs. O. did elaborate on the subject by explaining that true heavenly music is not at all like the music of Richard Wagner but closer to "Somewhere My Love," "Freight Train," and "Glow-worm."

13. Case of Mrs. N.E.C. Mrs. C. wrote about her experience of hearing an orchestra of violins playing for "hours and hours" as she and her husband drove in their car. Since none of our cases was of such long duration nor could percipients generally identify specific instruments, this case was rejected.

14. Case of L.M. Mrs. M. sent in a real "thriller." It seems the narrator tried to pick a water lily growing by a quicksand pit. As she was "slowly being sucked down and was in it up to my shoulders, I began to hear the sweetest music this side of heaven." Mrs. M. did not explain how she was saved from the quicksand. In fact it actually is almost impossible for a human being to be "sucked" into quicksand, despite the erroneous image given by the movie industry.

15. Case of J.P. Mr. P. claims to have heard psychic music when at a lake resort. It was a sweet female voice. Mr. P. drove home, the voice singing all the while. He then wrote out the music and offered to send me a copy. Mr. P. also has recorded the song and claims it has the ability to lift depression.

16. Case of Mr. E.C. This correspondent sent in a brief note to the effect that his departed friends and relatives often send him music.

17. Case of Mr. R.C. Mr. C. sent in an account of a materialization that sang to him at a séance.

18. Case of Mrs. N.S. Mrs. S. wrote me that every night she

hears singing in her kitchen, often of "There's a Garden to View for Me and for You Going Home." Mrs. S. also said she was a psychic and offered to give me a reading. She wrote that her husband has worked in a nuclear plant for thirty years, while, in fact, such plants have not been in operation that long. Some of Mrs. S.'s music also sounded like bagpipes. Hardly celestial.

19. Case of M.V.D. Mr. D. wrote of a haunted apartment where Caruso's voice sang.

20. Case of Mrs. M.C. Mrs. C. wrote of the music (church bells) she heard and also that she was the new Messiah for the "outer space" people.

21. Case of Mrs. M.P. Mrs. P. sent me an eight-page auto-biographical letter describing her pianistic talents, which she thought "psychic." She also sent me her hand print.

22. Case of Mrs. G.M. Mrs. M. sent a narrative of hearing music "of a full symphony orchestra" during an illness. Since the music was heard along with "visions" and "colors" that "whirled around her" as if "in a dream," the experience was probably caused by delirium.

As can be seen, these pseudo cases have little in common with the ones we used as genuine examples of the phenomena. Of the twenty-two cases which were rejected, only two mentioned the crescendo effect of the music and only three described it as beyond earthly music—the two major patterns which we uncovered. Also, the outlandish accompanying material disqualified many. I should note that the British cases did not seem to have these peculiarities, and thus a greater proportion of them were used. In reviewing my file of cases received for use in *NAD*, I find that some reports were disqualified for being too fragmentary or without detail, but not for the obvious reasons which made the above accounts unacceptable.

Appendix B

The Western Tradition of Astral Projection

Most persons intrigued by psychic matters have naturally turned to Eastern cultures and religions to find ancient doctrines more-or-less suitable to their awakened interest in psychic matters. And indeed, Eastern religions, more inherently "mystical" than the religions patronized in our own culture, do offer a rich psychic and metaphysical heritage from which to draw meaningful and fascinating doctrines on psychic phenomena. Even the psychologist and ex-president of the Society for Psychical Research, Robert Thouless, makes no secret of his belief that modern parapsychologists should orient themselves to the meditational methods of the Eastern religions (such as Yoga) in hopes of procuring better laboratory evidence of ESP.[1]

However, our own Western culture-base has also produced some striking doctrines on psychical phenomena—and the Greek philosophers, notably the neo-Platonists, came up with theories on astral projection not only concordant to even older teachings from the East, but parallel to the more empirical data imparted by such habitual astral travelers as Sylvan Muldoon and Oliver

---

[1] Thouless, Robert: *Experimental Psychical Research* (Baltimore: Penguin Books, 1963, pp. 124–25).

Fox, and researchers Hereward Carrington and Robert Crookall. According to a vast majority of occult writers, the astral body is not the actual "soul," but the "soul body." This same feature may be found among various Greek writings which discriminate between the "spirit" (pneûma) and the spiritual body (sôma pneumatikón). Another teaching to be found in popular occult lore, Eastern religion, and even mediumistic communications, is that man not only has a physical body and an astral body, but also a "fluidic double," a semiphysical cohesive which, during life, keeps the physical and astral body united and in coincidence and which is shed at death. This identical theme may be found in the *Pistis Sophia*, which differentiates between the "pure spirit" and the "counterfeit spirit," which seems to be subtle references to the astral and fluidic bodies. Centuries before, the Egyptians had written of the *Ba* and *Ka*, also the astral and fluidic bodies.

According to Robert Crookall, perhaps the greatest living authority on astral projection, the death experience is one and the same with astral projection; death is merely the "final projection." In his volume *The Supreme Adventure*, Dr. Crookall (formerly Principal Geologist of the London Geological Survey, and Demonstrator in Botany, University of Aberdeen) analyzes the death experience from various angles: persons having had spontaneous out-of-the-body experiences, persons having had the experience close to death (e.g., some having technically "died," only to be revived moments later), and those who did die and have communicated through mediums. All the testimonies agree on several components of the death experience. One such feature is that at the time of death it takes this dense "fluidic shell" three days to disintegrate, during which time the astral body, being enveloped by this shell, enters into a misty dreamlike state before it may progress to the "other-world." These data match perfectly with the testimony of the *Tibetan Book of the Dead*, which talks of a three-day misty swoon (Crookall has called it the "Hades" condition). And what of the Greeks?

The Greek philosopher Porphyry (233–304 A.D.), writing in

158

his exposition on Plotinus, states that an overly sensuous or impure spirit (which has an ultradense fluidic body, according to Eastern tradition) must, when detached from its physical body, be laid in Hades because it is too attached to the "moist spirit," as Porphyry calls it. Mediums have stated that debauchees remain "in the mists" for longer periods of time because of the initial inability of the fluidic double to disintegrate, which would allow the astral body to be released.

Another Greek philosopher, Philoponus, who sought to reconcile the philosophies of Plato and Aristotle, also noted that man has an immortal element or "soul," surrounded by an apparitional body which, however, persists only a limited time after death.

On this same theme, it is amazing to note the number of projection cases recorded by Robert Crookall which describe seeing a misty lake or river over which they must cross during their experience. M. Gifford Shine, the housewife who so many years ago became one of the first to write of her astral projections, in *Little Journeys into the Invisible,* describes this river in the same manner as many persons having had spontaneous projections with no other knowledge of the subject at all. Curiously enough, not only do the Greeks employ this symbol in the mythical river Styx, over which the dead must pass before entering Hades, but Porphyry, writing on Egyptian mythology, explains that the Egyptians drew supernatural beings as traveling on barges gliding over a sea not as a literal representation, but as a description of superphysical bodies traveling "the moist" or Hades realms between Earth and the "other-world"!

Again, according to Robert Crookall, if the astral body (normally invisible), is projected *along with* the fluidic double, this "composite double" will become visible. The Greek Stoics, according to Porphyry, maintained similarly that sensuous persons when leaving their bodies often attract the "moist spirit" to precipitate about them, thus making them attain some solidity and become visible. Such beings, at death, might become ghosts. This concept is little different from the present-day popular spiritistic theory of hauntings. It should be noted that Crookall

159

drew his conclusions from the records of spontaneous out-of-the-body experiences and not from the Greek philosophers.

In reviewing all the three hundred and eighty-two cases recounted by Crookall, we find that several narratives (sixty-three, to be exact) include instances of seeing either the dead or "helpers," discarnates who aid in the process of astral projection. The philosopher Philoponus wrote but a few hundred years after Christ that with the help of "daimons"—supernatural beings—the astral body could be made to appear for a short time.

The relation of the astral body to the physical body has instigated many writers to thought. Some years ago E. Thelmar wrote a book called *The Maniac*, in which the author maintained that her bout with insanity was caused by her astral body not maintaining proper coincidence to her physical body. Even as sophisticated a writer as Dr. Crookall has suggested that this imbalance might be the cause of some insanity. Philoponus wrote that what he calls "derangement" was caused when "the spirituous body either undergoes a certain breakdown or, by being out of symmetry, troubles and hampers the understanding," and attributes this notion to Aristotle. Philoponus also gives credit to Aristotle for the teaching that the astral body (ánō) is transparent.

Yet another Greek philosopher, and the most mystical of the lot, was the neo-Platonist Damascius (sixth century A.D.) who wrote of the "radiant body" (the equivalent phrase with that found in the *Tibetan Book of the Dead*) in his commentary on Plato's *Parmenidēs*.

Therein he attributes the astral body with luminescence. This statement is also to be found in the Tibetan scriptures and modern mediumistic communications. Damascius also wrote that, if the astral body becomes more material (enveloped by the fluidic double), it will lose this brilliance. This is quite in keeping with traditional testimony. The Greek philosopher also noted in his *Life of Isidorus* that some doctrines have it that the "radiant body" is shut in the head of the physical body. This is a notable statement, since many persons having had astral

160

projections have described the experience as of popping out through the head (often also symbolized by the vision of gliding through a tunnel).

It must be agreed that these allusions to astral projection and the belief in an astral counterpart to man's physical body are scattered and opaque; but they are definite enough to make certain correlations to other allusions and teachings in different cultures. It is hard to account for all the data on the grounds that the knowledge of the East was brought to the Greeks through missionary activities. The *Tibetan Book of the Dead* is one of the few Tibetan Tantric scriptures not "borrowed" from preexisting Hindu or other Indian sources, and was probably not even written down until about 700 A.D., after most of the Greeks had already written out their philosophies. However, the Tibetan doctrines and Hindu teachings probably do antedate them.

Our own culture sprang from the Mediterranean civilization. And like the East, it offers us a banquet of psychic writings. Perhaps if we were to take our eyes from the mysterious East for but a few moments, our own psychic heritage would become self-evident.

Appendix C

Ancient Doctrines of NAD

The word NAD, which we have so prodigally employed, is an ancient Sanskrit word—being the base sound of the universe. Similarly the "music of the spheres" was a descriptive title employed by Pythagoras to denote the cosmic sounds of the heavenly bodies as they fly through the infinity of space. These two titles represent only two of the ancient doctrines of supernatural music. Since this book, as was the previous one, is primarily a parapsychological thesis, we have spent little time on the musical aspects of the phenomenon.[1] However, in this appendix, I think we should indicate the great universality of tenets that would show that the universe is the embodiment of mystical sounds.

For instance, there are several doctrines that show a belief that the universe itself was created by sound. The Egyptians in their complex mythology believed that the world was created by the voice of their god, Thoth. The ancient Persians also believed that the universe had an acoustical base: They taught that the

---

[1] Some of the musicological implications of the phenomenon are touched upon in Professor Ian Parrott's review of *NAD* in the *Journal: S.P.R.* (March, 1971) issue.

163

first "cause" in the universe was sound, which became light, which gave birth to matter, but that, all in all, these transformations still had a base sonority.

Such doctrines as these were also found in early Christian teachings. In Chapter 7, I theorized that psychic music was actually an archetype of earthly music. The Christian Byzantine community likewise believed that all earthly music was an attempt to imitate the divine songs of praise sung by the angels, inaudible to human ears but sometimes giving rise to the inspiration of the early hymnographers.

In primitive animistic cultures, it is often maintained that all spirits have a specific sound and that only through sound can man communicate with the gods.

All these ancient doctrines suggest that music was considered inherently magical by early cultures. However, it was only the Greeks who suggested that certain individuals might be able to hear this music. It is logical to suppose that these early doctrines were formed by empirical observations of the NAD music and were transformed from a psychical phenomenon into a supernatural doctrine. As J. Combarieu has stated in his classic *La Musique et la Magie:*

> . . . in all known civilizations music has been believed to have a divine origin. Everywhere it has been considered not as a creation of man, but as the work of a supernatural being. There is nothing similar in the history of art or drawing. Naturally, man has given to music itself the power he attributed to the gods.

Standard theories as to the origin of music do not take this significant pattern into account. We now have empirical data to the effect that persons have heard divine music which has no earthly source. So have many ancient cultures also taught a doctrine of a supernatural musical force in the world. Because of the closeness of these two sets of facts, a cohesive theory can be made by joining them.

What is even more significant is that this concept of supernatural music did not disappear and was still found in more sophisticated cultures. Based on Pythagoras's concept of the "music of the spheres," Boethius (A.D. 480–524) wrote that music could be classified into three categories: music of the physical world, music of audible tones, and music of the human soul and body—again a reference to a metaphysical basis of music. Boethius's treatise, "De Institutione Musica," became the most prominent thesis of its day and continued to be so up to the medieval time.

Combined Index of Cases

ACKNOWLEDGMENTS

I would like to thank many people who helped in the writing of this volume: the editors of *Fate,* through which I gathered many of the incorporated accounts; and especially Mrs. Blanche Fortier, librarian of the Society for Psychical Research, who helped me obtain those cases from early issues of *Light,* and for sections of Ernesto Bozzano's monograph on death and psychical phenomena. I am also very much indebted to Renée Haynes for translating some of the accounts from French sources. And, of course, I would like to acknowledge my debt to all those who submitted their firsthand accounts and responded to my follow-up inquiries.

BIBLIOGRAPHY

Barrett, William. *Deathbed Visions*. London: Methuen, 1926.
Bayless, Raymond. *Animal Ghosts*. New Hyde Park: University Books, 1970.
Beard, Paul. *Survival of Death*. London: Hodder & Stoughton, 1966.
Bozzano, Ernesto. *Phénomènes Psychiques au Moment de la Mort*. Paris: Alcan.
"Census of Hallucination," *Proc.: S.P.R.*, Vol. X.
Crookall, Robert. *Events on the Threshold of the After-Life*. Moradabad: Darshana International, 1967.
————. *The Interpretation of Cosmic and Mystical Experience*. London: James Clarke, 1969.
————. *More Astral Projections*. London: Aquarian Press, 1964.
————. *Mechanisms of Astral Projection*. Moradabad: Darshana International, 1969.
————. *The Jung-Jaffé View of Out-of-the-Body Experiences*. London: World Fellowship Press, 1970.
————. *Out-of-the-Body Experiences: A Fourth Analysis*. New Hyde Park, N.Y.: University Books, 1970.
————. *The Study and Practice of Astral Projection*. London: Aquarian Press, 1964.
————. *The Supreme Adventure*. London: James Clarke, 1961.
Crookes, William. *Researches in the Phenomena of Spiritualism*. London: James Burns, n.d.
Elliott, G. Maurice. *Angels Seen Today*. London: 1919.
Findlay, J. Arthur. *The Way of Life*. London: Psychic Press, n.d.
Flammarion, Camille. *Death and Its Mystery* (3 Vols.). N.Y.: Century Co., 1921.
Franchezzo. *A Wanderer in Spirit Lands*. Chicago: Progressive Thinker Publishing House, 1901.

173

Fryer, A. T. "Psychological Aspects of the Welsh Revival," *Proc.:* S.P.R., December, 1905.

Gurney, Edmund; Podmore, Frank; Myers, F.W.H. *Phantasms of the Living*. London: Kegan Paul, 1886.

Hamilton, T. Glen. *Intention and Survival*. Toronto: Macmillan Co., 1942.

Hamilton, Margaret. *Is Survival a Fact?* London: Psychic Press, 1969.

Hart, Hornell. *Enigma of Survival*. Springfield: Charles C Thomas, 1959.

————. *Toward a New Philosophical Basis for Parapsychological Phenomena*. New York: Parapsychology Foundation.

————. "A Chasm Needs to Be Bridged," *Journal:* A.S.P.R., 1968, Vol. LX, No. 4.

————. "Scientific Survival Research," *International Journal of Parapsychology*, Vol. IX.

Hill, J. Arthur. *Man Is a Spirit*. New York: Doran Co., 1918.

Hilton, John. *Dying*. Baltimore: Penguin Books, 1967.

Holt, Henry. *On the Cosmic Relations* (2 Vols.). Boston: Houghton Mifflin, 1914.

Home, D. D. *Incidents in My Life*. New York: A. J. Davis & Co. 1864.

Hyslop, James H. "A Case of Veridical Hallucination," *Proc.:* A.S.P.R., 1909.

————. "Visions of the Dying," *Journal:* A.S.P.R., October, 1918, Vol. XII, No. 10.

James, William. *Varieties of Religious Experience*. New York: Modern Library, 1902.

Johnson, Raynor. *Watcher on the Hills*. London: Hodder & Stoughton, 1959.

————. *The Imprisoned Splendour*. New York: Harper, 1953.

Knight, David (ed.). *The ESP Reader*. New York: Grosset and Dunlap, 1969.

Lepp, Ignace. *Death and Its Mystery*. Toronto: Macmillan, 1968.

LeShan, Lawrence. *Toward a General Theory of the Paranormal*. New York: Parapsychology Foundation, 1969.

Light in Our Darkness. London: Psychic Press, n.d.

Marryat, Florence. *The Spirit World*. London: 1894.

Mead, G. R. S. *The Subtle Body in Western Tradition*. London: Watkins, 1919.

Morton, Rose (Pseudonym). "Record of a Haunted House," *Proc.:* S.P.R., Vol. VIII.

Osis, Karlis. *Deathbed Observations by Physicians and Nurses*. New York: Parapsychology Foundation, 1961.

174

Owen, A. R. G. *Can We Explain the Poltergeist?* New York: Garrett Publications, 1964.

Philip in the Spheres. London: Psychic Book Club, n.d.

Podmore, Frank. *Modern Spiritualism* (2 Vols.). London: Methuen, 1902.

Price, H. H. Presidential Address: S.P.R., 1939.

Randall, Edward. *The Dead Have Never Died.* London: Allen & Unwin.

Rogo, D. Scott. "Astral Projection in Tibetan Buddhist Literature," *International Journal of Parapsychology,* Vol. X.

———. *NAD: A Study of Some Unusual "Other-World" Experiences.* New Hyde Park, N.Y.: University Books, 1970.

———. "Content Analysis as Evidence in Parapsychology," *Parapsychology Review,* Vol. 2, No. 4.

Roll, W. G. "The Psi Field Theory," Presidential Address: 7th Annual Conference of the Parapsychological Association.

Salter, W. H. *Zoar.* London: Sidgwick & Jackson, 1961.

Sampson, Martin. "When the Curtains of Death Parted," *Reader's Digest,* May, 1959.

Shirley, Ralph. *Mystery of the Human Double.* Reprint, New Hyde Park, N.Y.: University Books, 1965.

Stace, W. T. *Mysticism and Philosophy.* Philadelphia: J. B. Lippincott Co., 1960.

"Starr Dailey." *Release.* Arthur Jones, 1959.

Stead, W. T. *The Revival in the West.* London: 1905.

Sudre, René. *Treatise on Parapsychology.* London: Allen & Unwin, 1960.

Techter, David. Review of *NAD, Fate,* April, 1971.

Terhune, Anice. *Across the Line.* New York: Dutton, 1945.

Toynbee A. (ed.). *Man's Concern with Death.* St. Louis: McGraw-Hill, 1969.

Tudor-Pole, W. *Private Dowding.* London: Watkins, 1919.

Tweedale, Charles. *Man's Survival of Death.* London: Grant Richard Ltd., 1909.

———. *News from the Next World.* London: Rider.

Tyrrell, G. N. M. *Apparitions.* Myers Memorial Lecture: S.P.R., 1942.

———. *The Nature of Human Personality.* London: George Allen & Unwin, 1954.

Watson, Albert. *The Twentieth Plane.* London: Sampsenhamm Marston & Co., n.d.

Wydenbruck, Nora. *The Paranormal.* London: Rider & Co., n.d.

Younghusband, Francis. *Modern Mystics.* London: John Murray, 1935.

Also Referred:
Atlantic Monthly, March, 1879.
Fate, July, 1969; April, 1971.
Forum of Psychic and Scientific Research, December, 1933.
Journal: A.S.P.R., Vol. XII, August, 1907.
Journal: S.P.R., Vol. IV.
Metaphysical Magazine, October, 1896.
Proc.: S.P.R., 1911.
Zeitschrift für Parapsychologie, March, 1933.

Printed in the United States
216482BV00001B/18/A